T0162725

INSIDE THE FIRE

MY STRANGE DAYS
WITH THE DOORS

BY
B. DOUGLAS CAMERON
WITH
DAVID R. GREENLAND

authorHOUSE®

AuthorHouse™
1663 Liberty Drive
Bloomington, IN 47403
www.authorhouse.com
Phone: 1-800-839-8640

First published by AuthorHouse 9/1/2009

ISBN: 978-1-4490-2200-6 (e)
ISBN: 978-1-4490-1275-5 (sc)

Library of Congress Control Number: 2009907706

Printed in the United States of America
Bloomington, Indiana

This book is printed on acid-free paper.

To Ray and Barbara Cameron

You showed me the way.

Untitled #1

Sometimes I watch you
When you don't know I'm there,
And I feel the love filling my eyes.

I saw your face when you thought
No one could,
And your sadness tore me apart.

Now I've hurt you
And I sit alone,
And remember the look in your eyes.

I hear a sad song,
About a lost friend,
And the tears begin again.

If I could hold you now,
And tell you I love you,
I'd give everything I have.

Because I saw your face
When you thought no one could
And your sadness tore me apart.

Brier Frasier

CONTENTS

PRELUDE   ix

PART ONE: INSIDE THE FIRE

  1. FROM ZYGOTE TO TROOPER   3
      (Or WHO IS THIS DOUG CAMERON ANYWAY?)
  2. NOVEMBER 3, 1968   10
  3. LETTERS FROM VINCE   16
  4. JUNE 14, 1969   25
  5. THE SONIC ORGASM   28
  6. DOUG CAMERON, ROAD WARRIOR   31
  7. LOS ANGELES: JUNE 16, 1969   34
  8. THE WORKSHOP   37
  9. MEXICO   42
10. MY SWIM WITH JIM   49
11. ELIZABETH   54
12. THE END   56

PART TWO: AFTER THE FIRE

13. "MAYBE FIND IT BACK IN L.A...."   89
14. THE COURSONS   99
15. VINCE TREANOR REVISITED   102

PART THREE: THE Q-95 CAMERON/MANZAREK INTERVIEW

16. December 11, 1984   119

ALMOST FAMOUS: THE DOUG CAMERON BANDS   144

EPILOGUE   148

POSTSCRIPT: THE SEARCH FOR MY ORIGINS   151

ACKNOWLEDGMENTS

First of all, I would like to thank Ernie Stokes of Rockford, Illinois, for reading through every early rough draft and being so helpful in the writing of my book. Ernie was one of my English teachers at West High School, and I consider him to be one of my mentors. The man's got SOUL.

In addition, I would like to thank: Flo Angileri, who, as my typist, struggled to read my frightful handwriting; Pat Boyd of Elkhorn, Wisconsin, who gave me a great deal of help restoring old photographs; I owe a special thanks to Gordy Moscinski for digitizing most of the photographs in the book; Dave Ross, Mike Andrew and Steve Connell for much moral support throughout the years; Todd Stokes for all of his artistic efforts and interest in the book; Joe Marola of Classic Color; Bill Cornman of realeyes; Cathy Borchmann, who helped immeasurably with translation and aesthetic considerations as well as editing; Greg Williams gave me some good suggestions (he's also a great friend—and my drummer); Marcos Lara for a couple of good ideas; Brier Frasier for the use of her poetry; Susan Franklin and the rest of the staff at AuthorHouse in Bloomington, Indiana; and to my students and staff at Guilford High School in Rockford— what a great group of people. Next year, more love, less politics.

This book could not have happened without the hard work and expertise of my good friend David Greenland. His previous authorship and extensive experience in the world of the printed word has helped me much in the final crystallization of *Inside the Fire (My Strange Days with the Doors)*. Dave's father refers to him as "Mr. Almanac." Having worked with him for the last few months, I can attest to the accuracy of this moniker. The cat is a walking encyclopedia of film, television and rock 'n' roll knowledge. It's been a pleasure to work with you, Dave.

I would especially like to thank my long suffering wife, Fran. She's been along for part of the rollercoaster ride, and there have been several difficult twists lately. Fran was raised in the city of Chicago, where she took a bunch of lemons and made some Andersonville lemonade.

Finally, thanks to Oliver Stone for the likeness of Val Kilmer as Jim Morrison in the 1991 film *The Doors*; Vincent Treanor III for helping me fill in the blanks; Penny and the late Corky Courson for permission to use portions of our phone conversations from 1981. And to the Doors themselves, living or dead: You haunt me every day of my life.

* * *

PRELUDE

BAM!

The snare drum shot crashed through The Shack restaurant. Then the organ riff ran through the cycle of fifths, sounding like a Hoover vacuum cleaner that had been transformed into a full orchestra. The last chord of the progression shifted from major to minor, the rhythm from straight 4/4 to a Latin style. A haunting baritone voice began singing:

> "You know that it would be untrue
> You know that I would be a liar..."

The table where a fifteen-year-old Culver Military Academy trooper sat munching a cheeseburger suddenly became a rollercoaster car. There was no "Please Remain Seated" sign hanging overhead, but even if there had been, I would have ignored it. I shot to my feet and raced over to the corner jukebox. The source of this magical music:

> "Light My Fire" / The Doors

The rollercoaster car started its rapid ascent. My life would never be the same...

* * *

I'm a piano player. A piano player is not to be confused with a pianist, for the two are quite different. Truly, a concert pianist is a musician with incredible talent and the Spartan discipline for not only practicing countless hours on end, every day, but also the nerve to sit at a monster grand piano before LARGE audiences and play classical compositions which everyone has heard MANY times before. As a pianist, love for the music he is playing has to outweigh his fear—even terror—of possibly not performing the music to perfection. And of being JUDGED.

On the other hand, there is the piano player. Of all the musicians in America, there are more piano players than any other kind. Most piano players play by reading music, but probably half of them also play by ear. By choice, I am one of the latter. Why should I bother reading music when I can usually play a piece after simply hearing it?

Music was my first love. One day, when I was about four, my parents were sitting in our living room at 1245 North Church Street in Rockford, Illinois, when suddenly they heard the sound of a piano coming from the large four season porch at the back of the house. I believe the first selection I played was a commercial jingle for Hamm's beer that I'd heard on television. Most people of my generation will remember the melody of the ad for the regional brew if they grew up around the Illinois/Wisconsin border.

We had a monstrous old upright piano on the porch, positioned against the inside wall. I would lift up the front cover of this immense sound kaleidoscope and play for hours, watching the hammers go in and out, making all these fantastic sounds as I struck the keys. I could create music without knowing how to read it.

As a piano player, I became good because I just loved playing, and this intuitive, inexplicable gift had an inner voice that overrode those of my parents, who bitched and moaned about my playing by ear instead of learning to follow the notes in those cheesy books that old Mrs. Haggstrom gave me. After roughly five years I became so sick of her lessons and practicing scales that I just had to quit.

When I saw Mrs. Haggstrom many years later, she remarked, "You were always up off of the bench, bouncing around." (As much candy as I ate back then, it's no wonder I was bouncing from the bench, off the walls…)

Mrs. Haggstrom never took me seriously as a pianist. I remember having to ask her if I could participate in a mass recital at the Mendelssohn Club, a dignified performance hall located in downtown Rockford. After she finally relented, I played some cross-handed drivel entitled "L'Avalance," complete with a number of mistakes. The two hundred or so people in the house might have clapped more enthusiastically if I had bent over and farted instead!

Through the drudgery of those early lessons I persevered and, with the help of my inner voice, became a piano player, not a pianist. But I have the Beatles to thank for rescuing me musically. While most people remember *The Ed Sullivan Show* of February 9, 1964 as the first time they heard the spearhead group of the British Invasion, I had seen them on television the month before—January 3, to be exact—when a clip of them performing "She Loves You" had aired on NBC's *The Jack Paar Program*. "You've got to see this," Paar told the viewing audience. It was a "WOW!" moment: A wall of screaming girls, jelly beans pelting the stage, and whatever music could somehow be heard amid the chaos. It was an entirely new sound, and like millions of others, I was floored. My inner voice told me I was finally hearing not only lovely music, but *fun* music, and it sent me rushing back to the piano.

The Beatles also rejuvenated a popular music landscape that had been slipping into bland mediocrity after the U.S. Army drafted Elvis Presley and Buddy Holly was killed in a plane crash. Of course, the Beatles were not solely responsible for the musical Renaissance that began in 1964. In addition to Britain, there were great tunes coming out of Detroit, Memphis and Chicago. I would have to include New York in this mix. As for Los Angeles, it would soon develop a scene of its own, producing the most popular and dynamic American band of the decade: The Doors.

This book was born to answer two questions I've answered hundreds of times over the years:

1. How did you get a job working for the Doors?
2. What was Jim Morrison *really* like?

It finally occurred to me that there was enough in my memory bank and personal files for a full account of those heady, strange days, the purpose of which is to illuminate the extreme good fortune of a young piano player who was initially mesmerized by the music of the Doors in 1967, and then, through the proverbial twist of fate, found himself in their employ two years later.

In addition, there were events I witnessed and learned of that I've never seen recounted in any of the seemingly endless books about the band or Jim and his tempestuous soul mate Pamela Courson. Take, for instance, the oddly polka-dotted blue-green rug I noticed when I first set foot in the Doors' workshop in West Hollywood. What were all those spots?

I suppose it is a tribute to my own strong will and musical spirit that I didn't become a complete goon or zombie when I first started listening to the Doors. I remained myself. However, there can be no doubt that I was captivated, totally impelled to take the musical journey the band prescribed. The Doors made more sense to me than anything else I had ever experienced. The sound really got to me first, but a few nanoseconds afterwards, the lyrics—poetry, actually—sealed the deal. What a fantastic combination of words and music…I loved it.

But, okay, let's be honest. There are a number of tunes in the Doors' catalogue which, although not pop fluff, cannot be called earth shattering. Most of them are at least fun. Some are awe inspiring. I believe that after "Light My Fire," my favorite would be "When the Music's Over." I know the guitar solo is really two tracks overdubbed, but I've never heard Hendrix, Clapton or even Jimmy Page sound like…*that*. Also, the guitar solo on "You're Lost, Little Girl" is gorgeous. Who else but Robby Krieger can touch it? Another of his tour de forces was 1968's "Spanish Caravan." I feel that one should have been extended, possibly signaling a dynamic new direction for the band, which at the time they sorely needed. The album it appeared on, *Waiting For The Sun*, was spotty in quality, a definite disappointment after the brilliance of their first two efforts.

The Doors, in 1968, were the most popular and arguably most important band in the land. Their controversial single "The Unknown Soldier" was banned by many radio stations, stalling at #39 on the charts, but its follow-up, "Hello, I Love You," became their only #1 hit a few months later, the fifteenth best-selling single of the year and outselling the Beatles, the Rolling Stones, Cream and Steppenwolf. Similarly, *Waiting For The Sun* was to be their sole #1 album, twenty-fourth among 1968's top fifty long players, though ranked behind Cream, the Jimi Hendrix Experience, the Beatles, Bob Dylan and Steppenwolf. (Proving that quantity does not necessarily equal quality, *Strange Days,* in my opinion their finest work, is also their weakest seller.)

The Doors ended 1968 with "Touch Me," the last Top Ten hit of their career (#3), as well as their most unusual. Not only did the band augment its sound with horns and strings for the first time, even Morrison's vocal was something of a departure from past performances. Frank Sinatra and Elvis Presley, the best popular singers of the twentieth century, also happened to be Morrison's favorites, and this was reflected in the vocal style he brought to "Touch Me." Producer Paul Rothchild felt Morrison was a great crooner, obvious on such earlier tracks as "The Crystal Ship" and "You're Lost, Little Girl," which Morrison hoped Sinatra might cover.

Although I could not have been aware of it, when I joined the Doors' road crew in the spring of 1969 the future of the band was very much in question, and the atmosphere surrounding Morrison & Co. was often less than comfortable, to say the least. By then Jim was more than bored with being a rock star and would have preferred singing blues tunes in some roadhouse dive. But only when he felt like it. In truth, he wanted to simply concentrate on his poetry and be taken seriously in that vein. And to have the ominous specter of the infamous "Miami incident" disappear. More on that later…

In 1969 the Doors were replaced as America's favorite band by another quartet, Creedence Clearwater Revival, who in that year alone released three albums and racked up such classic hits as "Proud Mary," "Green River," "Bad Moon Rising" and "Fortunate Son." But judging by the size of the crowds that attended the concerts I worked, the Doors' popularity remained huge. The band, however, paid a heavy price, as did at least one fan.

I never told any of the Doors about Cindy Sciacca, but I believe everyone should know what happened to her. She was a lovely freshman who attended West High School in Rockford, Illinois. And died at the age of fifteen. One night she placed the Doors' first album on her turntable, set the needle down on "The End" and took a bottle of pills. She never woke up. I didn't know her. Her class was a year behind mine. The school memorialized her with a page in the yearbook. I realize it wasn't the Doors' fault that Cindy died, but the incident illustrates what I've told people for many years: When one listens to the Doors, listen with a reasonable amount of common sense. The Doors are capable of conjuring up deep, dark forces in the human psyche. Jim Morrison would be the ultimate example. Jim Morrison was possessed by more than a few demons. This I firmly believe. As the German philosopher Friedrich Wilhelm Nietzsche observed, "When you peer into the abyss, the abyss peers into you." Jim Morrison peered.

As for myself, I feel fortunate to have worked briefly with the Doors and, unlike a long list of others, escaped the fire largely unharmed. And I now feel ready to tell the tale of my strange days and nights with Jim Morrison, Ray Manzarek, Robby Krieger and John Densmore. The rollercoaster is once again ready. The ceremony is about to begin.

Doug Cameron
Rockford, Illinois
May, 2009

* * *

PART ONE

INSIDE THE FIRE

– 1 –

FROM ZYGOTE TO TROOPER

Or

WHO IS THIS DOUG CAMERON ANYWAY?

Our grey stucco home was located in a beautiful older neighborhood on Harlem Boulevard in Rockford, Illinois. Across the street was a small Civil War monument, a large rock upon which had been bolted a bronze plaque commemorating Camp Fuller, a Union base located along the nearby Rock River in 1862. I saw that monument every time I went out front to retrieve the mail.. The rock never changed, nor did the contents of our mailbox, which was usually stuffed mainly with correspondence for my father, a district sales representative for Continental Steel of Kokomo, Indiana.

There was no reason to expect the mail to be any different one day in November 1968, probably the seventeenth or eighteenth. I idly thumbed through a dozen or so letters, the last one addressed to me. I couldn't believe my eyes…a legal size envelope, white in color, with parallel green lines on the left edge which included the logo: The Doors 8512 Santa Monica Blvd. Los Angeles, California. I tore the envelope open and was stunned to discover that I was being offered the position of assistant road manager! (Over the years, this significant piece of correspondence mysteriously disappeared in the accumulated dust of time.)

It was a lengthy letter, the first of seven I would receive from Doors road manager Vincent Treanor III, informing me that the job paid the princely sum of $60 per week, plus room and board, for my efforts. The amount wasn't much, but so what? The primary condition of my employment was that I first finish high school. Unfortunately, life at West High by this time was quite a strain because I had a very strong case of senioritis.

Like most parents would, mine questioned the wisdom of allowing their teenage son to tour with a rock band, particularly the Doors, but Vince called and talked to Dad about the gig. The terms were agreed upon, but I still had to finish high school. UGH! What a trial. Especially geometry, which blew me out of the water. Bud Chamberlain, a math teacher at West as well as a great guy, agreed to tutor me. Even with his help I barely passed the final exam. Who said musicians are good with numbers? Oh, by the way, I needed that geometry class to graduate. I squeaked through by one point. Never give up!

So who is this Doug Cameron, fledgling Doors roadie, anyway? Where did he come from? How did he reach this enviable position in America, circa 1968?

I was born in a crossfire hurricane. Wish I could say that. It sounds good, doesn't it? But it's not true, at least not physically. Spiritually and emotionally, however, it is. A young woman named Margie Allison and her boyfriend, Ed Johnson, shared some backseat time in a 1947 Packard—or it might have been a DeSoto—somewhere in a frozen field south of Russiaville, Indiana. I started out as a zygote. Phonetically, zygote sounds a lot like the German words *sei Gott*, which means "be God." I keep trying not to Be.

I was born on October 4, 1951, in Terre Haute, Indiana. Terre Haute is French for "high ground", and that might be closer to Heaven than I'll be when I drop to room temperature at some date in the hopefully distant future.

None of Margie's family were around to help with my entrance into the world. Approximately 140 miles to the north in Kokomo, Indiana, her people weren't even close. They sent Margie to Terre Haute so no one in Kokomo would know she had "a bun in the oven," as the ancient adage goes. I learned later that Ed was somewhat angered by the news of my existence. He told Margie not to try pinning any responsibility on him, and that he would tell everyone she had slept with all of his friends if she named him as the biological father. With that he quickly departed to begin an academic career at Bradley in Illinois. He was reportedly about 6'2" tall and had blue eyes and reddish blonde hair. I figure he must have been a Valkyrie, in Norse mythology a chooser of the slain, because he decided my fate in very short order. At least he set the stage. Goodbye, Ed…

Margie had a rough time the day I was born. In other words, mine was not an easy delivery. Years later I was told that there were a lot of screaming blue jays providing an accompanying chorus in the trees outside the hospital window. Pretty birds, but mean. By mistake, a nurse brought me to Margie, and when the blunder was discovered I was whisked away to a crib in another room. I was ON MY OWN. Not even a day old. Ain't dis a bitch? At least I wasn't a zygote anymore…just an orphan. Or as the French would refer to me, a bastard. Is it any wonder I have never been crazy about the French?

Within two weeks—or three, tops—through the help of a doctor in Kokomo, I won the biggest jackpot of my whole life: I was adopted by Ray and Barbara Cameron, also of Kokomo. The size of the jackpot? Incalculable. If it had been $500,000,000 I wouldn't have traded. Not then, not now, not ever. Suffice it to say that I felt very loved as a child. Very safe, very secure.

Both Barbara Cooper Cameron and Raymond Lindley Cameron were erudite, educated, lovely people who fell in love with me at first sight. Mom came from an old Fremont, Ohio family, and her great grandfather, W.E. Haynes, fought for the North in the Civil War. My dad's family didn't have any money, so his was an uphill battle not only in his family but in life as well.

We moved to Rockford, Illinois, sometime in 1953. Back then, Rockford was one of the country's leading manufacturers of machine tools and the second largest city in the state, outranked only by Chicago, located some ninety miles to the southeast. Today, Rockford is Illinois' fourth most populous community, and due to a failure to diversify its products and services through the years, leads in virtually nothing.

I was raised an Episcopalian, and through that experience can corroborate the conventional line regarding Anglicans (another term for Episcopalians) being chilly. They are. Mom used to drop me off for Sunday school at Emmanuel Episcopal Church and drive away. There I was, walking through this massive, foreboding building, searching in near darkness for the right room. Well, I just split. I started walking home, stopping at some old woman's house to ask directions. I wasn't much more than four. It's a wonder some wicked witch didn't snatch me up for her cook pot.

When I was six-years-old, my mother asked, "How would you like to have a little sister?" I remember my first reaction being, "Oh, no!" Something was going to threaten my position as Golden Boy of the entire universe.

Nonetheless, my sister Martha, whom we later dubbed Mardi, arrived one day in a bright blue blanket. She had a beautiful smile, a dimple and blue eyes. I thought, "Well, the blanket is the wrong color." I felt just like the character in the Andrew Gold tune "Lonely Boy" from then on. Over the years I treated my sister like crap 80% of the time. Today I'm lucky she doesn't hate me completely. On one level, I think she does.

My early years were very similar to millions of other boys growing up at that time in the Midwest. Bicycles, ice cream cones, a fascination with the old guns and helmets our fathers had brought home from World War II and/or Korea. I once spotted a Nazi helmet on the sidewalk in our neighborhood. No one around… Although tempted, I left it there. Had my conscience pulled me in the opposite direction, that helmet could have become the first piece in my current collection of military artifacts.

My friends and I spent many an hour at Sinnissippi Park, playing golf in the summer and sledding down a steep hill covered with deciduous trees in winter. Today no one sleds there because too many knuckleheads ran their sleds into trees. And with the ever growing abundance of lawyers and litigants, the city closed the hill. It was the city's fault a kid cracked his head open on a tree? The city did this on purpose? Kill all the lawyers?

As a youth, Jim Morrison was fond of pelting other kids with rocks, a sin of which I was guilty on at least one occasion. A friend and I were checking out a bridge being rebuilt on the Rock River when I decided that throwing some rocks at a couple of older guys was a great idea. The missiles didn't hit their targets, but the damage was done. With the angry kids in pursuit, we raced down a temporary wooden bridge only to discover that it had been partially dismantled. To escape we had to jump down from a height of over twenty feet. As I hit the ground, my right knee came up so hard that my jeans made a large scuff mark on my face. No broken bones, luckily, and my friend was unscathed. "Let's get the hell out of here!" I shouted. We did. Close call…

When I was twelve Mom and Dad finally told me that I was adopted. I don't remember this sudden revelation having any immediate emotional impact, but it may explain why seventh grade was ghastly. Real *Blackboard Jungle* time. Multiple classrooms, lots of street smart hoodlums with slicked back hair and cigarettes, all collected in a huge three story brick building called Roosevelt Junior High. (Ironically, I later became a teacher in huge buildings with multiple classrooms. The students' slick backed hair was gone. But not the cigarettes.) Many mornings found me in a fetal position on a bed in the nurse's office. The pain in my stomach felt as if someone was stabbing me with a knife. Gastritis. I hated Roosevelt. My grades were poor, and I nearly caused my father to have a nervous breakdown. His job gave him enough pressure without having to worry about me.

John Kennedy was shot that year, 1963. A Catholic family across the street was torn up. Kathy Earp, the oldest of the then six kids, stayed in bed crying and crying for three days. The nation was in shock. As so many others have said, America lost its innocence the day JFK was assassinated. No one could trust the government anymore because there was so much suspicion that Kennedy's death had been an inside job. Lee Harvey Oswald did it, we were told. One man, one gun. Still don't know for certain, but for what it's worth, I firmly believe Oswald did it.

Sadness hung over the country like a monstrous fog until that early February evening in 1964 when the Beatles performed on *The Ed Sullivan Show*. All that screaming…what a release! No more John Kennedy, but now there's a John Lennon. From a national tragedy to a national orgasm. The fog lifted. The music played. And in the summer of 1965, Jim Morrison and Ray Manzarek, sitting on a beach in Southern California, began planning their assault on the history of popular culture. I truly don't remember much of what I was doing that summer, but a year later, as the year-old Doors (still unknown outside Los Angeles) were perfecting their initial repertoire in such clubs on the Sunset Strip as the London Fog, Gazzari's and the Whisky-A-Go-Go, I distinctly recall Doug Cameron, not yet fifteen, being BORED OUT OF HIS MIND!

Diversion came in the form of military school. Yes, military school. What would Jim Morrison, rebel son of a naval officer, have thought? Or Robby Krieger, who also had done time in military school as a youth? Needless to say, I never told either of them about my mandatory three summers at Culver Military Academy, for which tuition was Big Bucks.

It so happened that my maternal grandmother, whom we called Nana, had quite a few extra shekels and offered to send me to the summer version of Culver, located near Knox, Indiana, in the northern part of the state. Nana's sons—my Uncles Dick and Jack—also spent a trio of summers there, beginning in 1939. Considering how restless I was, this proved to be a particularly propitious opportunity, even though I wasn't much of a joiner. Good thing, then, that the summer term at the academy was not as strictly regimented as the winter.

To be honest, I was indifferent regarding Culver, but my dad was quite excited. He had known about the academy as a young man, but his economically challenged family could not help him realize his dream of going there. Now his son, through whom he vicariously lived a great deal of his life, could attend.

Fortunate sons from across the country—actually the Western Hemisphere—descended upon the time-worn, tradition-tested shores of Lake Maxincuckkee to become plebes, members of the military's freshman class. The youngest enrolled as Woodcrafters, or as we older plebes called them, Wood Tics. Otherwise, one could join either the Naval School as a midshipman, as my Uncle Jack had, or become a trooper in the Black Horse Troop, which was Uncle Dick's choice, and mine. The latter was the School of Horsemanship, which taught young knuckleheads the finer art of equitation and allowed an aspiring trooper to savor the admonitions of a retired Army officer, namely the unforgettable Colonel Robinette. Robinette was a portly, pasty faced, bespectacled soldier who was never seen without his campaign hat fitting so snugly on his head that the brim was only millimeters above his glasses. He rarely failed to remind us that, "You don't have to be a bonehead!" We certainly benefited from this type of instruction. Oh, yes…

Troopers were quartered in very old wood-framed tents with canvas roofs and sides, screened windows and a screen door attached with a long spring that pulled the door shut with a loud slap anytime someone entered or exited. These tents were our homes for the next six weeks, so I heard that door slap *a lot*.

Again, Culver wasn't cheap, and I was never more impressed with that than when, on the first day of camp, I walked from the Quartermaster building to the troop area with a huge pile of brand new uniforms stacked high across my outstretched, straining arms. My campaign hat was a felt affair with a wide brim that made me look like Dudley Do Right. I was also issued khaki shirts and pants, blue blazers, blue chambray shirts, blue/grey riding breeches with a yellow stripe running down each leg and, as we were taught the English style equitation, a pair of impressive tall, black boots that came all the way to the knees. The plebes looked somewhat like Nazi officers—young ones—and were not in any way familiar with the system. They couldn't march, always complained, didn't like to stand at attention, and liked to shovel horse crap even less. With 150 horses stabled in the riding hall, there were *plenty* of road apples.

Every horse had a name, and the one I remember most was Clock, being ridden that first year by Jay Gillogly, Squadron Commander of both troops—A and B—for the "final make" of summer '66. Every week there was a new make, where various first and second classmen would receive lower or higher marks based on their new job for the next week. If one was a "dick off"—as a guy named Pete Schulz-wenk was fond of calling troopers who behaved like jerks—he would be made Stable Officer or Mess Officer, in charge of the chow hall detail. The latter was definitely preferable to the former.

Another bit of terminology that Schulz-wenk loved was "little birdies." "Where are my little birdies?" he would shout with a somewhat arrogant air when commanding a group of plebes who couldn't tell their asses from a hole in the bottom of the Zuider Zee.

Pete's brother, Axel, was a fellow trooper of mine in Troop B, but I remember the Schulz-wenk parents more than the boys. Herr and Frau Schulz-wenk were very cultured, internationally seasoned and obviously Germanic. They had blonde hair and piercing blue eyes. The father, an industrialist, was a CEO of Volkswagen Brazil. He had a Ph.D, as well as an especially penetrating gaze.

I once asked Herr Doktor Schulz-wenk, "How do you say 'will' in German?"

"I can't understand you vith dat gum in your maus."

"Sorry…"

Axel told me that not only had his father been the commander of a tank battalion on the Eastern Front in Russia, his grandfather was a major bigwig in the early Nazi party. Axel's father died in 1971, leaving behind much wealth. Evidently Pete came by his condescending attitude naturally.

MANY years later, after I'd become a self-educated scholar on the Holocaust, I read a book about the death camp the Nazis maintained at Treblinka in Poland and came across a section about Franz Stangl, the camp Kommandant. It was none other than a certain Doktor Schulz-wenk who gave Stangl a job at Volkswagen Brazil, after the war. Schulz-wenk was one of the most powerful men in South America, and that job allowed Stangl to avoid capture and prosecution for war crimes for several years. Schulz-wenk *must* have known who Stangl was.

Ashley Ward III, whose father developed and owned the Winnebago Recreational Vehicle Company, was my tent mate that summer of '66. He was from Ohio and quite a guy. In fact, there were a number of good natured guys at Culver, good natured despite being dumped there for the summer by wealthy, aristocratic families who wanted to boast that their sons were at one of the most prestigious college preparatory academies in the country. The Black Horse Troop in particular was noteworthy for usually participating in almost all the presidential inaugural parades in Washington D.C. That was until Bill Clinton.

The list of wealthy kids was long: Will Kieckhefer, whose father owned Mercury Outboard Engines; Phil Kresler, Doctor Lock Kresler's son from Kentland, Indiana, and Jim Short, whose father was the hardboiled assistant base commander of the Strategic Air Command base at Columbus, Mississippi. And then there was Steve Somerall—fun, gregarious and anything but a snob. I respected that, and remember him for another reason in particular.

Summer '67: My second at Culver, and a colorful space in time the media dubbed The Summer of Love before it was even over. Steve and I were riding our mounts at a slow walk down an Indiana back road late one hot morning in early July. My butt was starting to hurt.

"So, somebody said that you play a mean piano," Steve remarked.

"Been playing since I was four," I replied. "Never played in a band, though."

"You ever heard of the Doors?"

"No, I haven't."

"Well, hell," Steve exclaimed. "They've got a huge album out with some of the most contorted, dynamic, deadly rock and roll ever."

I suddenly remembered the song I'd heard on The Shack jukebox the day before. "Oh, yeah! The Doors! Man, that 'Light My Fire' really rattled my grates yesterday!"

"That's only the short version," Steve said. "It's longer on the album. You should check it out."

Indeed…

Not all of my summer memories are of Culver. In 1967, while the World's Fair was being held in Montreal, my family went on a fishing trip to Grindstone Lake in Ontario. The following year, we drove out west with another family whose father owned a Buick dealership. Consequently, we rode in a brand new Buick Skylark station wagon. (Remember station wagons?) I vividly recall first hearing Iron Butterfly's one and only hit, "Inna Gadda Da Vida," blasting from the car radio, as well as a catchy ditty called "Hello, I Love You" by none other than the Doors. I was back on the rollercoaster…

* * *

– 2 –

NOVEMBER 3, 1968

There's no question whose idea it was to take the bus into Chicago to see the Doors. It was mine. I had been hanging around with Steve Connell, a classmate of mine at West High., Class of '69, so I asked him to take the trip with me, and he agreed.

Steve was a tough kid with blonde hair, glasses and a rather weather-worn, angular face. He was around six feet tall and had the biggest knuckles in Rockford, due to his study of karate. He obviously spent many hours pounding boards to abuse his knuckles into a permanently swollen state. It was just implied, if you knew him, that big hands were critical to being perceived as dangerous. The "King of Bad" at West was a cat named Norm Stanley, when Steve and I were juniors. Norm was a black belt and let everyone know it. Steve tried to emulate Norm. Years later Norm and I discussed what it meant to be considered "bad." "Yeah," Norm said, "I thought I was bad until I walked out of a restaurant one night and two guys beat the holy crap out of me."

Steve and I caught the bus from the old Greyhound Bus terminal on the east side of town, just east of North Second Street. The day was chilly, but not biting, and the sun was out. On the way to Chicago, as we careened down Interstate 90 at approximately 200 feet per second, we discussed various girls we knew, which ones we lusted after, and the ones we didn't. We were both old enough to have experienced problems with the opposite sex.

Eventually the conversation moved to the wild rumors we had heard about Jim Morrison's stage antics. Once, at a rock concert in nearby Belvidere, a guy told me that someone he knew had seen Morrison pissing on some amplifiers. Wow! Was this cat Morrison out there.

We got off the bus around 12:30 p.m. and headed down to the Coliseum on South Wabash. Steve wore an olive drab Army surplus fatigue jacket, while I had on a Navy blue cotton shirt. We were both wearing blue jeans. Neither of us knew shit from Shineola.

We purchased our tickets from a nondescript woman in a glass enclosed booth at the south end of the foyer, then walked thirty or forty feet to the north end and started pulling on the handles of the twenty or so doors facing us. As we moved left to right we discovered all of them to be locked—except for the very last one. I pulled, and it opened with very little effort.

Steve and I entered and "OOHED" and "AAHED" at the size of the hall, which had a seating capacity of probably around 10,000. The place was empty except for two people on the stage adjusting a white drum kit that included an unusually large number of tom-toms, at least five. As we made our way down to the stage, we were approached by a man with dark shoulder-length hair and an Army jacket similar to Steve's. I thought, *Oh crap, he's going to kick us out.*

Instead, he greeted us with, "Hi, guys. How ya doin'?"

"Good," we chirped in unison.

"Well, look, I work for Triangle Productions and need some help setting up spotlights. How would you like to make a couple of bucks?"

"Sure!" He didn't need to ask us twice.

"All right, come with me."

We followed this cat and passed through some drapes to the right of the stage, then down a concrete passageway to a small room where the spotlights were stored. For the next couple hours we walked up and down dirty, rickety stairs that reeked of puke in several places to set up the lights. The work wasn't exactly fun, but time passed quickly.

"What's the name of the opening act?" I asked the stranger.

"The Holocaust."

His answer bounced off my psyche and threw more fuel onto a flame that had been burning in me since the age of four. Other than music, I had developed a fascination with the past, specifically the dark side of history. The Holocaust, so many genocides. I have never been able to escape my obsession with the Jewish people. Why can't they find peace? They certainly deserve it. There is not room enough in this book for a delineation of my searching and the answers I have found thus far. Besides, that's another story.

"The Holocaust," I mumbled. "That's an odd name for a band."

Back on the main floor the stranger reached into his pocket and gave us each $3.00.

That's not much, I thought to myself.

"Look," he said. "Take these buttons." He handed us two very small white buttons, the same type used by political candidates. "Put them on your collars. They're backstage passes. How would you like to meet THE DOORS?"

Holy crap! my brain shouted. But I said, "Yeah, that'll work."

Steve was grinning like the village idiot.

We never did find out who the stranger was.

We walked through the passageway and down to an underground parking area. There were a few people standing around, mostly hippie types, and as we were chatting with one of them, a huge U-Haul truck, probably a ton and a half, came roaring through the large opened overhead doorway on our left.

"It's Vince Roadie," the hippie said.

"Vince Roadie?" I asked.

"No. It's Vince, the roadie for the Doors."

"All right," I said to Steve. "Here we go."

We walked over to the driver's side of the truck. Sitting in the cab was Vincent Treanor III, hired as the Doors' equipment manager roughly a year after he'd first seen the band in August of 1967.

"Hey, Vince," I greeted. "How ya doin'?"

"Yowser," he replied. "It's all good."

"Do you need any help setting up?" I asked enthusiastically.

"Actually, yes, I do."

"Sign me up, too," Steve said.

In short order, the back of the truck was opened. Steve and I saw a huge amount of equipment staring at us.

We're working for the Doors! I told myself.

The next couple hours were pure manual labor, lugging twenty or more Acoustic amplifiers onto the stage and strategically placing them where directed. Vince, who sang lines from various Doors tunes as we worked, was not the sort of individual I was accustomed to seeing in Rockford. He had a Boston accent and wore a chocolate colored two piece mod-cut suit with some white French collar-looking scarf around his neck. It was obvious to us that he knew exactly what he was doing, and about three and a half hours later most of the equipment was ready. Now it was just down to positioning things so the Holocaust could get on and off expeditiously.

Barney Pip, a deejay from WCFL who resembled a homeless person, came bouncing into our company as though blown in off the street. It seemed like he was on some speed, but he was friendly enough. The lights went down and Barney introduced the Holocaust to the audience, which over the past two hours had made the Coliseum a full house.

The Holocaust were loud, unimaginative and boring. (Shall I tell you how I really felt?) After an hour or so spent damaging the hearing of the people in the first ten rows, the band ended their set. As the house lights came back up, we helped them swiftly lug their stuff off the stage.

I was standing on the stage, looking back toward the underground garage, where I had noticed a dressing room—actually a house trailer—parked along the rear wall behind the stage. In the doorway stood John Densmore, the Doors' drummer, gazing out into the Coliseum. Then I spotted organist Ray Manzarek, attired as usual in a sport coat, and guitarist Robby Krieger. There was no sign of Jim Morrison.

Following my curiosity, I entered the cavernous garage—probably 150 feet across, 60 feet deep, ceiling so high as to be almost invisible—and noticed four beautiful girls surrounding a tall, long-haired figure who stood outside the trailer. He was wearing black cowboy boots, a light blue shirt with a collar and some sort of dynamic cut to the cloth, and an old pair of generic white Levis. His hair was dark and looked dirty, as if it hadn't been washed in a month. His handsome face was startling, like Jesus without the beard. His eyes were an uncommon blue, with a strong hint of Ireland, or maybe Scotland…out on the moors. There was no doubt—this was Jim Morrison, the self proclaimed Lizard King. At least that's what he dubbed himself at the conclusion of "Not To Touch the Earth" on *Waiting For the Sun* back in July.

As I started to walk over to Jim, a short and VERY rotund man wearing a leather hat and leather cape (which made the cat look like a monstrous cowhide mushroom) got to him first, a girl in tow. He attracted Morrison's attention and handed him a portrait he'd done of the Lizard King.

"How do you like it?" the mushroom asked.

Jim took a moment to study the artwork, then slowly drawled, "It's one of the best I've seen."

After the fat man and his girlfriend left, I sauntered over to Morrison, still standing in front of the trailer.

"Hi, Jim. I'm Doug Cameron and I have to say, I love your music."

"Nice to meet you, man. And thank you. Uh, listen…I gotta get a beer."

The subtext on his comment was probably *I've heard that 50,000 times before…Am I BORED yet?"*

Jim turned and stepped up into the trailer. I could hear the tab on a can of beer snap open.

I spied Ray in the immediate vicinity, and he was looking at me. I went over and handed him one of the new soft cover Doors souvenir books a Chicago printer had just delivered to the Coliseum. As Ray leafed through the booklet, Steve took a picture. In the shot I look like a typical teenager, holding my own Kodak Instamatic camera, never dreaming that it was the same one I would use when I went on the road with the band.

Ray was very cordial. I told him that I too was a piano player, and he said, "Practice makes perfect."

I didn't prevail upon him to sign the booklet for me, but I did ask John Densmore, who graciously sat down on the trailer steps and scrawled his name across his picture. Steve once more caught the moment on film.

A man of medium height with long, wiry light brown hair, psychedelic pants and a white T-shirt emerged from the trailer. Who could fail to notice the red Gibson Melody Maker guitar strapped around his neck? This was Robby Krieger. I boldly asked him to play something for me, and he obliged by running through the opening chords of "Light My Fire."

Two big black men, the Doors' professional bodyguards, suddenly appeared. They looked like Gayle Sayers in a suit and tie. They also looked pissed. I didn't say a word, nor did I see anyone else speak to them. As young as I was, I still knew they were more than likely packin' heat. They kept a close eye on me, as well as the beautiful girls—the groupies. Steve was able to take a couple shots of Ray and Robby waiting to go onstage before the bodyguards made us vamoose.

BOOM! Down went the house lights…and I mean down. I couldn't see my hand in front of my face. A spot hit Barney Pip and Jim's mic at center stage. I could sense the anticipation. There was the sound of movement in the hall, scattered screaming and war whoops. Pip made a few very brief political comments, then announced:

"Ladies and gentlemen, from Los Angeles, California…"

WHAM! Robby broke into "Back Door Man" and a scream that sounded like a man having his balls cut off ripped through the place. After that, nobody felt safe. The hackles on everyone's neck were raised. The spotlight hit Jim's face, and as he looked up, some in the audience had to wonder if they were seeing a god…or God?

The Doors ran through their standard twelve tunes, including "When the Music's Over," "Celebration of the Lizard," "Love Me Two Times" and "People Are Strange." Just before the concert began, Steve and I cleverly decided to go through the curtains and into the hall to take a few photos of the band in action. Guess what? Despite our little white pins, the police would not let us return to the backstage area. We had to find seats off to the far left. We were pissed.

Less than two months before, the Doors had blown the roof off the Roundhouse in London, but the Coliseum concert was lackluster. As I later learned, Jim had gotten drunk in Columbus,

Ohio, the night before and had a horrible hangover. During the show he just clung to the mic stand and sang with his eyes closed. I wasn't aware that Morrison's increasing fondness of the bottle was causing a great deal of tension within the band, and that he'd recorded his vocal for that year's "Five To One" totally smashed. The band played one long set, followed by one encore. As usual, it was "Light My Fire. And then it was over.

I felt lonely when I saw the four Doors walking to the limousine waiting for them back in the underground garage. Really lonely, as if a part of me had been removed. I may have felt worse had I known the tenuous state of the band. That summer, shortly after their acclaimed appearance at the Hollywood Bowl in July, Morrison told Manzarek that he'd had enough, he was quitting. Ray begged him to give it six more months. November 3, 1968, was the beginning of month five.

Steve and I helped Vince tear the equipment down and pack it back into the truck. Vince and I exchanged addresses, said goodbye, and Steve and I began our long walk to the bus station.

On the ride home, I looked out at the cold, dark, featureless Northern Illinois night, knowing that I had just experienced the most exciting adventure of my life. There was no way I could have known that the fates were quickly aligning to provide me with an inside view of a world that was beyond my wildest dreams. From inside a fire…

* * *

– 3 –

LETTERS FROM VINCE

(Reproduced as written)

Following are four letters sent to me (and my dad) by Vince Treanor III, the Doors' road manager, between November 1968 and April 1969.

November or December 1968

Hi Doug,

Well, I guess we really burned the wires Wednesday night. Thursday night we had our van stolen—from in front of our office yet—with over 2 cord boxes, 4 new PA columns and the 2 bass cabinets. The van and its contents were recovered within ½ hour but what a bad trip.

Anyway, I assume that by the time you read this you will have made some solid plans about school and the West Coast. I can only repeat my first words to you—first things first. Get school over with and go from there. I might sound a bit seditious but may I suggest you also start doing something really sincere about your draft. If you do not wish to be involved there are several legal, though not exactly accepted, means of obtaining either a 1Y or 4F status. I suggest you prepare now because you have only 1 year or less to prepare.

I am sure that by June some arrangements can be made for your employment in some phase of the music field. However, may I suggest that in the mean time that you do some real hard work on your organ or piano practice. You do apparently have some talent. Why should it go to waste?

You are obviously interested in music. You can channel this interest and ability into a very productive use by learning music theory and keyboard technique. Although it is not a surety that you can be a smash success in a group you can't even try if you waste your efforts. I think, as I mentioned in our conversation, that you can improve you talents musically and technically making chances for success in either field far more probable. This is obtained by taking lessons and sincerely and diligently practicing and by obtaining books from your electronic supply store [Ryder series Basic electricity Vol 1-2-3-4 Basic Electronics Vol 1.2(3?). Basic Volume 1 and 2 are good for starters] you can improve your technical knowledge tremendously. When can all this be done? Simply while your buddies are out "blowing" grass or drinking themselves into ill health insensibility and/or getting some chick pregnant you can be doing some homework. While they are wondering how and why you obtained an important position with some groupie, musical or technical, you can be satisfied in the knowledge that though you may have missed what is currently considered to be "pleasure," "fun," "groovey" type action you have gained knowledge and experience valuable to you for all of your life and without which you can never hope to get any really good position with any group.

Concerning Christmas vacation—I am sure that IF you do your absolute best—and no less—in school, be on the best of conduct—that which would indicate to you sincerely concerned parents that they can have confidence in your judgment and sensibilities—that you and your parents will work some equitable plan. They are as human as you, but you are young and without too much experience. Seek and ye shall find, knock and it shall be opened to you, ask and it shall be answered.

Well, think things over a bit, find your sense of values if you are able and work things out. Keep in touch by all means. If you are able to visit here, try for December 26th—January 1st.

Vince

* * *

Sunday, 12-29-68

I got your letter today. I arrived back in L.A. last night and was met by warm air and a gentle rain in some respects quite a contrast to the cold sleet I left in Boston. It was too bad that you couldn't visit here for vacation but consider that the guys are taking it a bit easy and nothing is really going on. You might have been disappointed in life out here. Best to save it, Doug, and devote all your energies to School and your swimming. Keep your mind straight and stay out of social "entanglements." Doug, I think the best advice I can give you is to devote every effort towards finishing school. You have but 6 ½ months to go. Do not worry about what is now or what might have been "if." Just do your best towards school. That right now, is your job. Doug if you are to succeed in any venture you must never fail to remember that all of your mind and spirit and body must go into it. Set a goal for yourself—like graduating with a B or A average. Then set another goal—working with the DOORS. Then possibly another—college. Having set your goal make that your life. All else must come afterwards, each in order of importance. I am sure you understand. But one other thing You, especially at your age, must keep in mind. No matter how you try if pleasures run your life—like dope, drinking, broads and smoking, your going to miss out somewhere. I will not allow a person using alcohol or dope to work with me. I am dead set against smoking, and no matter how well you do all else it's to no avail if you're a father—keep it where it belongs.

Anyway, we are on the final run to get the amps done for Madison Square Garden on Jan. 24th. That should be quite a show. I am not sure, at this time, whether or not we will be having other dates on the tour or not nor do I know when we will be in Chicago. I will let you know well in advance though.

Regarding this summer. As you know I have a helper now. I am not sure whether he will stay with me or not. In any case, when school is out and you can come out here we will arrange something. Whether it will be directly or indirectly with the DOORS I am not sure—time and circumstances will tell. It would be both impossible and unfair to promise your friend anything now. You realize he is available for only the summer and I need a full time individual. It is unfortunate but true that due to our current managers past experience with equipment that he does not allow that much for a helper for me now. I'm doing very well to get a helper an a miracle for 2, three—forget it! I am sure you can appreciate my position. I can do very little about it. We have to keep things on an even keel and I more or less have to be satisfied with what small gains I can get. We shall wait and see what develops for you. That, to me, is the most important. Others come after, OK? Well, I have to get busy. Keep in touch, Doug and work hard for your first goal.

Vince

February 21, 1969

Dear Mr. Cameron:

I received you letter a couple of days ago and now sit down to try
to give some andswers.

Doug is like many young people of his age. He has a hero, or a
circus, which he wants very badly. He is willing to work hard in
school and meet whatever other conditions which you might have set
for him in order to obtain his goal - namely working with, or some
reasonable approximation, the DOORS. It is true that we meet many
people in our travels. They even travel out here or call, or write.
The general run of these people are, however, dopers, disalusioned,
or detached from reality. Doug seems to have some logic up there
along with a great deal of youthful enthusiasm and driving ambition.
The only reason Doug might obtain his goal, unlike the others whom
we meet is that he is willing to work for it, and he is not involved
with drugs. I have dismissed two other assistants for this reason.
If he comes through with whatever his part of the bargain might be,
and you feel that he's intelligent enough to stay out of mischief
(Not that he would have that much time for it) then let himwork the
wanderlust out of his system. He has a big dream and this summer it
might be possible for him to travel to places which he may never
again have the chance to see. That alone will be a great experience.
It was for myself, as well as for the DOORS, a really wonderfull
thrilling experience to travel in Europe last September. I am really
looking forward to Japan and Australia (I'd really enjoy seeing the
aborigiones make it rain ((Spelling?)) and a return to Hawaii.

This bring us to other things - at this time we have no definite
scheduel except for the period, mid June to mid or late July.
The current plans are Japan first then Australia, then Hawaii and
back to L.A. about 4 to 6 weeks. Doug will receive $60. cash plus
his travel and expenses while on the road. If we work a spare job
he will get a split (This related to doing sound work for other
groups on a contract basis). Living accomodations will be arranged
with a friend of mine who has a large apartment. This will be suitable
if Doug plans to stay for a matter of a few months. We will make
other arrangements if the stay is longer. The chances are fairly good
that we will be in amplifier production then and if this is so he
will be getting 80 to 100 per week.

8512 Santa Monica Boulevard • Los Angeles, California 90046 • 659-1667

As all parents do, I am sure you are somewhat worried about what sort
of mischief he can get into while away from supervision. May I assure
you that I am dead set against drinking smoking, and the use of drugs
in any form. I have dismissed 2 assistants for just this reason. He will
be limited in his ability to travel free since transportation on his own
will not be easy, and he will have plenty to keep him busy. It will be
quite easy for you to get in touch with him at almost any given time
until we go on the read trips. I'm sure he'll be full of bounce for the
first few days but he'll calm down I'm sure.

Forthe present it would be advisable to obtain his passport,
This involved a certified copy of a birth certificate, passport ohotes
which are easily obtained from any photographer near the passport
office, and vaccinations along with the certificate signed by doctor
and health dept. Total cost is about $20. total time, including waiting
for the passport about a week or so. This should be done now, however,
to avoid any mishaps. His visas will be obtained here from the various
diplomatic envoys which require them. He should be advised that the
passport is probably, outside the certificate, the most valuable
document he will ever posses and it should be so treated.

Well I am not sure whether or not I have covered all the points but I
guess I came close. I hope that you will excuse the spelling and
typing errors. I use an electric typewriter here at the office and I'm
sure it hates me. Besides it's late and I have been squinting at
printed circuits in a silk screen stencil all day and I'm about blind.

Thank you for writing, Mr. Cameron, I hope that I will get a chance to
meet you personally sometime when we are in the area.
Detroit Olympia stadium 3/28: Cleveland Public Aud. 3/29: Cincinatti
Music Hall 3/30. There are no other dates schedueled nearerat this time
and probably will not be until after July. Feel free to write or call
at any time. Unless I'm on the road I can nearly always be reached at
the office.

       Sincerly,

       Vincent Treanor

8512 Santa Monica Boulevard • Los Angeles, California 90046 • 659-1667

Mr. Raymond Cameron

04-16-69

Hello Doug:

I felt that I might write to you after our conversation. To cover a few points which we discussed so that we are on the same plain, here's what goes now. We are going to New York one week from this Sunday do a TV show and will be back in town on the next Tuesday, I expect. Other than that, and a few minor incidents in the studio, we have nothing set for dates until June 28th when we will probably do Denver, Colorado. Our next scheduled date is in the Hollywood Bowl on July 5th, about a week later. This, by the way, is the first anniversary of the Bowl date of 1968. We have no real plans after that. There are several reasons. We may make the bowl date a farewell to the U.S. type thing and split to Europe where we will do England, France, Germany, Sweden, Denmark, Amsterdam, and possibly Italy and Spain. This tour will be about two months long, allowing for not only the playing dates but also for a vacation and a chance to see Europe again. After that we do not know. There may be a chance that we will follow on to Japan and Australia. This is highly speculative. At this point you know pretty well as much as any of us do except Bill Siddons who is, at this time, making plans for the European trip. It is highly doubtful that we will be playing anywhere in the U.S. until after we get back from Europe. This will give the courts time to hassle things and Jim time to prepare defenses as well as letting the press and public do a little reflecting on the state of things. With a good European tour behind us and hopefully a successful single and album having been released, we may well be back in everyone's good graces. The Miami incident will well serve to cool Jim down a bit, I hope. It was just one of these dates that nothing went right, tempers were frayed, and the arena in which we played was not really ready for us as such. This is not to deny that Jim went a bit out of line, but the general attitude of the southern mind did not help matters. Of course what went down from there is a matter of history. Hysterical reporters, who, by the way, have gone out of their way to try to make statements favorable to Jim as well as trying to cover for some of the things that they wrote—I'm sure they knew what will happen when we get our feet out of the mud—and the general public lost all sense of propriety and cool and said anything and everything that came to mind. It does seem strange that Jackie Gleason who is a woman chaser and an alcoholic should be on a stage cheering for "Decency." Mind you I have nothing against Gleason. I have met him personally and I really think that he's a right guy but He, because he makes all the adults laugh is excused for his immorality where Jim, because he is a long hair and entertains kids with song and words which are alien to the adult world cannot commit transgressions without being hounded by the general public and their minions.

Enough of that. I am glad that your folks have taken a second look at things and I certainly hope that their faith can be justified. Now to turn to you. I feel that from here on in the permission to come out here will be based on your scholastic and personal conduct. I hope that you do not forget this. I want you to also remember that, parents allowing, your stay out here will be governed by your behavior. Doug, I don't care what you have heard about L.A. and the people in it. I have no intention of having you come out here—at least to work with me—with the idea that you are going to blow it. You have slightly less than eight weeks to do your thing for your folks but I am expecting the same kind of behavior from you here that you would give your parents back home. I really mean that. Doping, drinking, and smoking are out. Don't forget that Jay was added to the list of casualties when I found out that he had taken dope. You are coming out here for a change of scenery and people, to sort of be on your own for a year to mature a little. If all works well you'll get quite a background of knowledge in the life of a performer and the problems that go with it. But this is not supposed to be the opportunity to get out from under your parents feet and just go wild by any means. I am not too happy with the thought that your parents are going to sort of expect me to replace them and that's the only way you'll be able to take this opportunity. But then I also feel that when I give a person the chance to work with me and assume some of the responsibility that goes with the job that they will be understanding of their position. I'm sort of putting my trust in you. Assuming your folks let you come out they are trusting you to keep straight and probably hoping that I'll crack the whip. Not really. I'm putting out the rules of the game and believe me if they aren't followed there is only one thing that will beat you back to Chicago and that's the telegram announcing your return. But I'm not going to be a substitute parent.

You did ask when you might be wanted out here. I don't know what the schedule is that I have written in here. We don't really plan on working too much between now and August. There is really no rush except that I may well be doing a great deal of PA work by then. I have begun to line up some jobs where I will supply the sound for the gig. It is lucrative but tough. Assuming all goes well with your end of the bargain I could say that you can come out whenever you like up to about the 20th of June. This, of course, assumes nothing else happens.

Well, I guess that's about all for now. Keep straight, Doug, Believe me I want no problems. Keep out of trouble at home—I know school is nearly over and it's coming spring and the tendency is to go out with the boys. Don't do it fella. You must uphold your parents trust if you wish them to give you freedom. You've had your swimming season and you're in good shape—you'll need the strength the big columns weigh 240 pounds each. Better get some weights and work out a bit. Ha! I'll let you know what develops here. By the way—for your parents benefit—Jim voluntarily surrendered for trial and is now on bond. We feel that there is enough evidence in our favor, and so little proof of the alleged acts, that we may have the whole case dismissed. Of course we are fighting against a prosecutor who has stated that he wants to use this incident as an example of what will happen to anyone who misbehaves in Florida, who has asked, in public statements, for the maximum penalties as prescribed by law (not fines but prison sentences) and these to be served consecutively NOT as in most cases concurrently (ask your Dad what this means) and all of this BEFORE JIM HAS BEEN PROVEN GUILTY in a fair (?) trial. You can see the thinking in that part of the country.

Well on to better things. Take care of yourself and stay straight—don't blow it at this late date—write to me as to what's happening up your way when you get the chance. As for me—back to the drawing boards.

V

• •

– 4 –

JUNE 14, 1969

It was raining on the night I vividly remember sitting in the car with my girlfriend Kathy. The raindrops etched lazy, meandering trails down the windshield as the sodium vapor streetlight tried to decide how to infract our vision. We were listening to Barney Pip on WCFL when we heard an ad for the upcoming Doors concert on June fourteenth. The announcer went through the usual spiel, then said, "So be at the Auditorium Theatre when James Douglas Morrison invites you to…"—the famous anthem kicked in:

"Come on, baby, LIGHT MY FIRE!"

I felt excited and sad at the same time. I really loved Kathy. She had my heart. Now I had to leave her. I graduated on June 6, 1969, and eight days later I officially became the first sanctioned assistant road manager for the Doors.

On the morning of June 14, Kathy, my parents and sister Mardi accompanied me on the drive to Chicago's O'Hare International Airport. We were to meet Vince and schlep the Doors' equipment over to the Auditorium Theatre. The band would be arriving later. We stood at the gate and watched passengers deplane, among them a longhaired, skinny cat in a bright royal blue velvet shirt.

It was Vincent Treanor III.

"That guy is as queer as a three dollar bill," Dad said.
"There's nothing you can do about it now," said Mom.
"I'm not worried," Dad said.

I introduced Vince to my entourage, and we made our way down to the baggage area. Vince's trick was to send all the equipment as baggage. That way we could avoid the heavier airfreight charges. This was indeed quite a feat because the Doors' gear, newly designed by Vince, weighed tons. Vince called the amplifiers "monoliths", the term inspired by the Stanley Kubrick film *2001 A Space Odyssey*, in which a mysterious monolith is found buried on the moon. Like that towering slab, the amps were very large, to say the least. When we wheeled them through airports we frequently heard people make comments about coffins. Each amp had a special black road case, and there were twelve in all.

As many books have mentioned, Vince was an electronics wizard, and on stage he was essential. He originally came from Andover, Massachusetts, and built pipe organs on the East coast. After moving to Los Angeles, he helped set up the first production line for Acoustic amplifiers. During the time I worked for the Doors, the first twenty Acoustic amplifiers ever made were stacked in the back room of the band's workshop. When the Doors broke up, their manager, Bill Siddons, sold all twenty, but to whom I don't know. The new monolith sound systems produced 5,000 watts RMS, enough to power a small radio station.

After saying goodbye to my family and Kathy, I got busy loading much equipment onto the truck Vince would drive to the Auditorium Theatre. Everything, even the transformers, had a special road case. At the venue, we were attaching aluminum heat syncs to the back of each amp when some cat named Bill wandered in, said hello to Vince and proceeded to help us set up, a process that usually took around two hours. As we worked, Vince mentioned that none other than Paul A. Rothchild, the Doors' producer, would be along for what was going to be a rather short tour.

Later, while I stood at the stage door (looking out into the alley) a Cadillac limousine pulled up. I could see a lot of hair inside. The Doors had arrived. They got out and greeted me. Jim was especially friendly and shook my hand. I reintroduced myself and he said, "Yeah, I remember." I doubted that he did. Everyone had more hair than the previous November, and Jim was sporting a full beard. In his suede leather jacket and matching pants he resembled a cross between Jesus Christ and Daniel Boone.

Out of nowhere, Paul Rothchild appeared. Rothchild, whom Ray referred to as the fifth Door, was the legendary producer responsible for classic albums by, among others, the Paul Butterfield Blues Band and Love, label mates of the Doors' on Elektra Records. He was short, balding and seemed very sharp.

Phil Kresler, my buddy from Culver Military Academy, was also there, at my invitation. He and I were asked to "go for" fried chicken for the band and milk for Rothchild. When we returned with the grub the opening act was in the process of doing a sound check. That's when I first met the Staple Singers, Pop Staples and his daughters. I believe his grandson was the group's drummer. They blended folk and gospel into a pleasing mix and were promoting their current album on Stax, *Soul Folk in Action*.

We delivered the chicken to the band, already finished with their sound check, and Phil was fairly well dumbstruck by the impression Jim Morrison made. "Those eyes..." was all he could say.

There was a special element added to shows this night because a very well known (and famously short tempered) light man who went by the stage name Chip Monck had agreed to handle the lighting for the tour. At one point during the first concert, Robby walked around behind the wall of amplifiers looking for something, bathed in a tremendous aura of blue light. Vince and I agreed that temperamental or not, Chip Monck was one hell of a light man. A couple months later he would be stage manager at the historic Woodstock Music and Arts Festival. His booming voice can be heard on the soundtrack.

The Staple Singers finished their set and received a very appreciative response from the packed house. Now it was TIME. Vince and I were positioned behind John Densmore's drum kit. The entire Auditorium went dark, but I could make out figures walking towards the instruments. There was tension in the air, this being the Doors' first performance since the infamous March 1 fiasco at Miami's Dinner Key Auditorium.

In the annals of "bad vibes" concerts, that event ranks second only to the disastrous Rolling Stones show at Altamont nine months later. Under the influence of alcohol and the outrageous antics of a confrontational group of thespians known as the Living Theatre, Jim taunted the audience, bringing the faithful to a full boil and infuriating the authorities. Based on the false charge that Morrison had, among other infractions, exposed his genitals to the crowd, a warrant for his arrest was issued. The trial date still loomed. In Miami's wake, spring concerts in such cities as Philadelphia, Toronto, Pittsburgh, Detroit, Dallas and Boston were canceled. Radio stations pulled the band's records from play lists. The two most recent singles—"Wishful Sinful" and "Tell All the People"—stiffed. Sales of the next album, *The Soft Parade*, which had taken an agonizing nine months to record, would be merely, in Ray's words, "so-so" when released in July.

Jim stalked out of the shadows and stood next to me.

"Lay it on 'em, man," I said.
"Do it," he exclaimed, invoking the title of a song on the upcoming album.
"Ladies and gentlemen, from Los Angeles, California…"
Robby tore off the opening riff of the as yet unrecorded "Road House Blues."
"…THE DOORS!"
"YEAAAAAHHHHHHH!" roared the crowd.

Everybody was on their feet. Jim walked to center stage, the spots hit him, and the masses understood. He had every damn one of 'em in the palm of his hand.

* * *

– 5 –

THE SONIC ORGASM

My mind wandered back, back before Kathy Aurit and her lovely brunette hair, back to a young spitfire of a girl that could wrap your soul around her wrist and make you feel like a charm bracelet: Jane Andrews. I didn't want to leave Jane for my third and final summer at Culver, but Dad had raised hell, so Trooper Cameron made the phone call and hooked up with camp registration. Jane and I had been virtually inseparable, driving around in Dad's white Mustang coupe, often rodding the piss out of it.

The dreaded Sunday finally came, and Dad and I hit the road for Culver. We arrived at tent city, unloaded my bags, shook hands and said our farewells. I didn't feel well. And the following morning…

"What the hell is wrong with you?" asked Phil Kresler, my tent mate for summer number three.

"I have an incredible sore throat," I croaked. "Can't even swallow. I'm going to the infirmary."

I was checked into the infirmary with a thundering case of mononucleosis and a temperature of 103 degrees. During my five weeks in bed, I dropped from 180 pounds to 155. I had to take two Darvon pills an hour before each meal just so I could swallow. The infirmary was not air conditioned, so I awoke many mornings in sheets soaked with sweat.

About three weeks into my illness, Phil visited and brought a toy for me, Mr. Mono—a switchblade knife he had picked up in Mexico. A couple days later, Mr. Mono unwisely decided to impress a nurse with the new plaything. As she stood over my bed, I whipped the knife out and snapped it open.

"What do you think?" I asked.
"Umm, you're not allowed to have that," she replied, reining in her shock.
"I don't care about it anyway," I said, closing the blade and handing it to her.
Where is Jane when I need her? I thought to myself. I remembered her charms. And her harms. Our relationship was like an equally balanced scale. She could make me feel like a king, and then tear my heart out.

"Trooper Cameron!" snapped the nurse.

"Yes, ma'am?"

"You are to report to Commandant Maull on Monday morning."

"Yes, ma'am."

Mr. Mono had recovered well enough by Monday to leave the infirmary and walk the two hundred or so yards to the Commandant's office.

"Trooper Cameron?" Commandant Maull rumbled.

"Yes, sir?"

"What are you doing with a switchblade in the infirmary?"

"Nothing, sir. It's not mine. A friend loaned it to me."

"Are you aware that this offense is grounds for expulsion?"

"No, sir."

"I have considered the matter seriously, and I have spoken with your father. I don't feel that your expulsion would serve any purpose. Your record otherwise is clean. I'm going to allow you to stay at Culver. I know you've been ill. You may not ride on the hike as your spleen might rupture. You will ride in the truck and perform light duty for the rest of the summer. Is that clear?"

"Yes, sir."

"Dismissed."

Damn that Phil Kresler and his knife! I swore to myself as I walked back to the infirmary. That was close! As I got back into bed, a new but familiar sounding tune sprang from the radio:

"Hello, I love you, won't you tell me your name…"

It sounded a bit reminiscent of "All Day and All of the Night" by the Kinks, a band I liked. But it was clearly by another band. My favorite band…

* *

FLASH FORWARD:

There were two shows at the Auditorium Theatre in Chicago on the night of June 14, 1969. The first was tentative, rusty, and the Doors were off. It just didn't click. However, the second show curled the hair of everyone in the first ten rows. Beyond the first ten rows, the audience experienced culture shock. No flash pots exploded, no one danced. During the dark epic "The End," Jim Morrison rolled on the floor, screaming and writhing in histrionic agony. Classic Greek theater performed by four fantastic musicians. The spectacle was DYNAMIC: a sonic orgasm.

The band walked off the stage to tumultuous applause. Phil and I accompanied Jim to the dressing room while the other Doors waited in the wings.

"We'll be your bodyguards," I told Jim.

"Where's the beer?" he demanded, then quickly found one.

I noticed that the entire building was literally vibrating, the crowd stomping their feet and chanting "DOORS! DOORS! DOORS! DOORS!" It was the only time I have ever been in a concert hall which humans could shake to its foundation.

Jim chugged the beer, then the three of us headed back to the stage. The Doors took their places, John Densmore struck the snare drum once, igniting "Light My Fire." The audience had an out of body experience. They were no longer a crowd. They became a congregation. I have never witnessed a moment when so many people expended their total energy for a common goal. It was like staring the spirit of America right in the face.

• •

FLASHBACK:

"Where are you going?" Phil asked.
"To the music building," I replied.

Now under the spell of the Doors—and in possession of much free time—I spent the remaining weeks of the Culver summer practicing piano. It was during this period that I became accomplished enough to improvise with my right hand independent of the left. I learned Doors songs, Beatle songs, and just songs I liked, all by ear. All self-taught.

Due to my illness, the summer as a military event was a bust. But musically, the summer of '68 was when I became a real piano player.

* * *

– 6 –

DOUG CAMERON, ROAD WARRIOR

Vince Treanor, Chip Monck and I got into the second taxicab. I had signaled the first cab, but some guy pushed me out of the way and took it.

"You fucked up, man," Chip said as he pulled out a stick of incense, jammed it into part of the cab's interior and lit it. Wherever he went, incense burned.

The cabbie began babbling on and on about some problem, so Chip tossed a ten spot at him and said, "Stuff it." The babbling stopped.

We arrived at the Astor around 1:00 AM. As if by magic, a sexy looking woman got on the elevator with us. She and Chip shot each other knowing glances that were beyond me. Vince and I took one room of the penthouse suite, which had twin beds, and Chip claimed the large bed at the other end of the suite.

Suddenly the phone rang. It was either Bill Siddons or one of the Doors—I don't recall—calling from the Playboy Mansion. He wanted us to join him, but Vince put a clamp on that idea. "We've got a busy day tomorrow. Way too much to do." So my one chance to experience Hugh Hefner's version of Paradise went up in flames.

I noticed a couple of suitcases and opened one to see who it belonged to. Inside was nothing but two bottles of vitamins.

"That's Robby's," Vince said.

I was amazed. The guy had brought along only the clothes on his back. Talk about traveling light…

When morning came, I walked into the darkened main room of the penthouse suite to find Ray and Robby asleep on uncomfortable looking trundle beds. Chip had just entered the bathroom, and on the far side of the suite I saw the woman from the elevator in the far bed. Naked. My, oh, my… Neither Jim nor John were anywhere to be found.

Before leaving the hotel we bumped into Paul Rothchild. He rambled enthusiastically about how there had been no distortion on Ray's organ during the concert. "Unprecedented," he said.

He obviously considered Vince's knowledge of sound systems to be nothing short of genius. I remembered Vince telling me that Jim was "intimidated" by the power of the new monoliths the first time the band used them.

It was fortunate that we got an early start that day because we needed the time. I always felt quite a bit of angst knowing that I shared the responsibility of setting up the equipment in every city the Doors played. At O'Hare International Airport, Vince pulled his usual stunt with the baggage and paid a couple airline handlers to grapple with the onslaught of gear. One guy was sweating bullets. "He's a drinker," Vince said. "You can tell when they sweat like that."

It was my turn to sweat profusely as we loaded the equipment onto the promo cargo truck at Minneapolis International Airport. By four o'clock that afternoon everything was dialed in for the band's sound check at the new Civic Auditorium in St. Paul.

Tony Glover, a sometime journalist and sometime musician, showed up and blew some harp as the Doors ran through a blues tune. Without warning, one of the speakers began a continuous screech. I grabbed some tools, but when I got to the amplifier in question Vince and Chip shoved me out of the way, jerked the offending speaker out and replaced it in a flash. Later, Vince said, "What were you waiting for, sonny boy? You've got to get it done quick."

He was right, I had to admit. I needed more practice replacing the speakers, which were 15" Altec-Lansings with a very heavy magnet on the back. They cost $125 each, and in 1969 that wasn't cheap.

During the sound check I happened to overhear a conversation between Jim and Robby.

"Listen," said Jim, "in 'Light My Fire,' when you do the riff at the end of the solos…"

"Yeah?"

"From now on, just do it six times, not ten. It's too much."

Soft spoken Robby mumbled something I couldn't hear.

The two shows that evening went fairly well. Nothing terribly memorable occurred, except when, during a blues number, Jim finished blowing his harmonica—an instrument he didn't play very well—and threw it against the rear wall of the huge stage. I was proud of myself for not going back to search for it. I'm sure someone found it eventually.

At the conclusion of the second show, as his band mates left the stage, Jim lingered and looked out over the diminishing crowd. He took the microphone in hand and asked, "Which one of you lovely young ladies is going to take me to dinner tonight?"

Predictably, a beautiful woman, probably in her early to mid-twenties and wearing a very revealing dress, tried to literally climb the stage, which had to be seven feet tall. Two cops stopped her. Jim turned and casually walked away. The woman, disheveled, walked away quickly, trying to restore her dignity.

We struck the stage—meaning that everything had to be taken down and packed away—and headed for the motel. Robby and John always roomed together, and Chip was still on board. Ray and Jim flew back to Los Angeles immediately after the concert. I hung around with Robby, John and Chip for a while, but really had no interest in what they were discussing—politics and bands I knew nothing about—so it was time for "lights out." Again, I had the wonderful opportunity to share a room with the 33-year-old Mr. Treanor.

* * *

– 7 –

LOS ANGELES

JUNE 16, 1969

Flying out to L.A. from Minneapolis I had the good fortune of sitting next to a very voluptuous blonde. (All voluptuous blondes eventually migrate to California, don't they?) Vince, of course, flew first class. We landed and left it to a trucking company to deliver the equipment to the Doors' workshop/office in West Hollywood.

My most vivid memory of that first day in Los Angeles is of Vince and I heading north on La Cienega Boulevard in a rented red 1969 Dodge van, seeing people dressed in such wild styles, and a tremendous number of interesting shops. And so many beautiful women, not all of them voluptuous blondes.

We arrived at the band's headquarters at 8512 Santa Monica Boulevard long before the equipment truck. The building, a two-story mustard-colored structure, was deliberately deceptive, with the word ANTIQUES painted in brown across the front. As much as the Doors appreciated their fans, they didn't want to be bothered at all hours of the day and night while trying to rehearse or conduct business. Around the corner was the new studio of Elektra Records—built largely with profits from the sale of Doors albums—and conveniently located near two of Jim's regular hangouts, the Alta Cienega Motel and The Phone Booth, a topless bar. He also kept an apartment on nearby Norton Avenue.

The building was approximately 35 feet across and 50 feet deep, with a small, acrid-smelling half-bath inside the front entrance. Beyond that was an electronics work room. Vince cautioned me to be careful when using the soldering iron in there, then showed me the bass drum head cover emblazoned with the Doors logo that he had made for the band's performance on *The Smothers Brothers Show* back in December. The offices were upstairs, the band's large rehearsal room downstairs. In the back was a long room that spanned the entire width of the building. This was where the twenty Acoustic amplifiers were stored. In the rear, a sliding glass door opened out to a very small outdoor expanse of fried grass and gravel. There were some wooden support poles for an upstairs deck—also very small—and under the deck lay what remained of a cannibalized Gibson Kalamazoo electronic organ. I was shocked to see that keyboard lying there, but I was to see more disturbing sights later.

After a long day, Vince and I jumped in the van and drove east from the workshop, then north to the Hollywood Hills. We took a winding route through several neighborhoods to 3220 Durand Drive, a studio apartment Vince rented from a rather nasty woman in her late fifties or early sixties. The location, however, was anything but nasty. Durand Drive ran along the highest crest of a hill, and the apartment had a huge picture window that offered a magnificent view of the sprawling Los Angeles basin below. The Capitol Records building was one of the closest recognizable buildings, and at night the city lights sparkled like a vast carpet of diamonds.

The only problem was the single bed, which I had to share with Vince. He was so odd, and I kept asking myself, "How could one person be so weird?" Then again, how weird were the Doors? They hired him. But who, exactly, hired *me*? The band? No, it was Vince. And the unadorned truth is, Vince was not heterosexual. He was enamored of muscular young men. Like me. He could also be quite devious. In one letter he asked me how Jim had taken notice of me, and why Jim had asked him to hire me. Vince knew no shame. The band members may have thought I worked for Vince, but as far as I was concerned, I worked for the Doors.

I spent that first night next to Vince, hugging the wall the whole time. The next night…

"Listen, Vince. This sleeping arrangement isn't going to fly."
"That's fine. We'll put the mattress on the floor. You can have that."
"Fine."

Life with Vince was trying at best. He somehow had the erroneous notion that I was going to be another of his male trysts. As it slowly dawned on him that he was with a heterosexual of some character, he resorted to different tactics. One night after supper at some restaurant (we never ate at the apartment), we were driving home when Vince decided to show me how frustrated he was by driving the leased red Dodge van as fast as he could up the hills and around the curves of Durand Drive. I just thought, *What a nut case!*

Vince's big passion was male models. He talked often about Steve Reeves, a body builder who became an actor, portraying such mythical hunks as Hercules. Another of Vince's favorite subjects was the quality of sperm and how I should do this and that to make sure that mine was just right. I ignored him.

He once asked to check my tan line. I wasn't wearing a shirt, but my pants were on, belt securely buckled. He grabbed my waistband and pulled it down a little bit to examine how my tan was coming along.

"I think that's enough of that," I said, backing away.

Vince was disappointed in me, but I could not have cared less. Truthfully, I was homesick as hell. I loved Kathy so much and she was two thousand miles away. I have to confess that there were many days when I cried in the shower.

Vince told me a little history of his time in the apartment. He had been burgled two times and lost quite a lot of stuff, including a large collection of early Doors photographs. He showed me a place in the closet where there was some type of projector.

"They missed this," he said.
"That's such a bummer about those pictures," I said.
"Right about that, Sonny Jim."
"Er—Vince?"
"What?"
"Don't call me Sonny Jim. My name is Doug."
"Fair enough."

I confess there were times I was alone in the apartment and snooped a bit. The most interesting item I came across was a letter in a nightstand drawer that was addressed to Jim from a Dalton Clarke in Florida. I guessed that Clarke was a relative, maybe Jim's maternal grandfather. The letter, written after the Dinner Key Auditorium on March 1, implored Jim to visit for a few weeks and try to calm down. How Vince ended up with this piece of personal correspondence I have no idea. But I shouldn't judge. I had no business snooping. Jim had most likely discarded it. There was a standing rule at the workshop—any time anyone called for Jim, especially his mother, we were to tell them that Jim wasn't there. I heard she called frequently, but I never talked to her. I felt then, and I still do, that being estranged from one's family just isn't natural. And there was something very unnatural about Jim Morrison.

* * *

– 8 –

THE WORKSHOP

One morning, early in my stay on Durand Drive, Vince's landlady needed to speak with him about something, so he and I went up the few steps to her house. She let us in, and while they were talking I glanced down at a table and noticed that she had copied my parents' address off of an envelope I had received the day before. I took this opportunity to "cancel" her ownership of the address. She immediately went on my SHIT list. I was in the process of assessing Californians, and she was quite an example. Many of the people I'd met or observed in Los Angeles seemed suspicious to me.

After grabbing breakfast at a Denny's, Vince and I went to the workshop and began making repairs to the monolith system, which was now unpacked and lined up against the walls of the main room. It was still relatively early in the morning, probably the Tuesday after the weekend concerts in Chicago and Minneapolis. Jim and an actor friend I hadn't met named Tom Baker, started up the stairs to the office. When Jim noticed us working, he came back down, walked over, looked me in the eye and asked, "What did you think of the Chicago concerts?"

"Well," I replied, "I thought the first one was rusty, at least not in a groove. But the second one…man, you guys leveled the place. I mean, not that you had to worry. You have a ton of fans in the Chicago area. I'm from Rockford, and when my friends at school found out I was going to work with you guys, it was like I was a god."

"Um-hmm."

From then on, Jim pretty much had my number. I was another one of the ASSHOLES who bought into all of this rock star crap. He was, or had to be, secretly duplicitous when it came to young, snot-nosed fans like me. On one hand, he relished the adulation, but on the other, he couldn't respect it intellectually. He wrote a poem about assholes that I read many years later, and he included himself in this grouping.

After I had placed my foot squarely into my gap-toothed mouth and nibbled for a while, I ambled away and got back to my general knocking about, trying to find something that resembled work.

"Are there any more warrants out for me?" Jim asked Vince.
"Not that I've heard, Jim. But we need to talk."

For the next hour or so I tried to keep my distance, feeling their conversation was none of my business. Tom Baker also tried to fade into the woodwork somewhere. Vince appeared to be really laying it on. Jim seemed to be doing a lot of listening. Once the presumed admonitions were over, Jim and Tom went upstairs.

"Did you hear any of that?" Vince asked me.
"No."
"Good."
"He needs to calm down," I said.
"Why don't you go out and wash the truck?"
"Right."

I would eventually learn what Vince and Jim had discussed. Thirty-nine years later…

For various reasons I would go up the stairs to the office, a very large room with two desks to the left of the entrance, a couch along the front wall to the right of a picture window, and on the far wall another couch. To the left of the window was a door to a small 8'x10' deck. This was where a sparsely haired painter named Leon Barnard worked when not taking care of the band's publicity. I don't know where he came from or where he went after the Doors broke up. No one ever told me much about him, but he was friendly enough, and I did see some of his artwork, now faded from memory.

Kathy Lisciandro, one of two secretaries, was the wife of Frank Lisciandro, Jim's UCLA film school buddy. I don't recall the name of the other secretary.

A door in the middle of the south wall led to the office of Bill Siddons, the band's manager. Siddons, not much warmer than an iceberg, was only four years my senior. The Doors definitely put their trust in young people. It always seemed to me that Siddons made every effort to separate Jim from the rest of us. Looking back, it was probably Jim's desire.

Mr. Siddons had a lot of energy and talked incessantly about BMWs. One of the first impressions I had of him was seeing him lying under his VW Minibus in front of the workshop late one afternoon. He was cussing up a storm and ripping parts from under the vehicle with his bare hands. These parts were then thrown into the closest lane of Santa Monica Boulevard.

One morning I was changing a speaker and looked to the right of the front door and saw two men talking. One was Bill Siddons. The other looked *exactly* like John Lennon! I had such a knee-jerk reaction that I stabbed a hole in the fabric of a $125 Altec Lansing speaker. Of course it wasn't Lennon, just some guy with whom Siddons had a business relationship.

Just before the second weekend of my employment, Mark Bolen, a cat Robby had met in Hawaii, showed up at the workshop. He had been in a band called Silver Bike, and he was allowed to have a whack at Robby's red Melody-maker guitar, strumming some uninspiring chords.

Suddenly, Vince announced that Mark and I were to deliver some of Chip Monck's lighting equipment to Monck's home in Mill Valley, where such rock stars as Janis Joplin lived. Mill Valley, a suburb of San Francisco, was only a "mere" five hundred miles north of Los Angeles, and it was already late afternoon. Vince gave us a credit card so we could gas up the van, but not one dime for expenses, one reason my diet in those days was so atrocious. (Chocolate milk and donuts for supper!) I had to resort to buying junk food with the meager amount of money I'd brought from Rockford. Although I was set up on the payroll, I had yet to be paid anything for my work. My first check was waiting for me on a Monday, but I had quit the previous Friday. More on that later…

Mark and I drove all night, and we didn't find Monck's house until three in the morning. A nameplate on the front door revealed that Chip's actual name was Hermann Monck. He wasn't home, but his wife was kind enough to invite us in. We took advantage of her offer to use the pool, and as we were swimming—in the buff—she made us some oatmeal. After wolfing that down, she gave us each a blanket and pillow and we quickly fell asleep on the floor of a spare bedroom. Good woman, though not the woman who apparently had spent the night with Chip in Chicago. Ahh, the rock and roll lifestyle…

We left shortly after and did a quick tour of San Francisco. Mark had been there before and knew his way around. We ate lunch in Chinatown, where I bought some incense and a burner.

We hit the trail, on our way to logging more than one thousand miles in two days, and stopped for a young brunette woman hitching her way to L.A. She wasn't feeling well and seemed to get sicker and sicker as we rode along. When we got to Los Angeles, Mark dropped me off at Durand Drive, exhausted, and drove off with the girl. I never saw either of them again.

The next Monday, the Doors scheduled a rehearsal at the workshop, minus Jim. Bored with Los Angeles, he had flown to New Orleans. That morning I saw John, Robby and some guy I didn't know standing outside the studio. John was talking enthusiastically about a recent Buddy Rich concert. Both he and Robby were big jazz freaks.

Robby showed me some copies of a couple Doors songs that a copyist had just dropped off. When the band finalized the arrangement of a number, a copyist was hired to put the music and lyrics on paper. And voila! A book of Doors music for people who either couldn't play by ear, or wanted to learn the exact chord changes. In my experience, most copyists usually get it wrong.

On this particular morning, Ray walked into the workshop looking dapper in a white shirt, slacks and sandals. As he and his band mates got ready to play I was chagrined to learn that I had to go with Vince to see some cat about repairing some of the monolith road cases. We also went to the Altec Lansing factory in Escondido for more speakers. By the time we returned to the workshop it was nearly three in the afternoon. Fortunately, Ray, Robby and John were still rehearsing. Vince went off somewhere to screw himself into a hole, and I sat down on a trunk to listen.

Jim had written the lyrics for "Land Ho," a song about seafaring and his grandfather, who was a sailor, and the others were attempting to hammer out an arrangement. They had just gotten to the part that went "I've got three ships…" and John was trying to decide what to do with the drums.

"Why don't you do some rim shots there," I suggested. "Like you do on 'Light My Fire'?"

John thought about it for a nanosecond, tried one or two snaps on the rim of the snare, then dismissed my idea. At least I actually had an opportunity to help compose a tune, and it was indeed fun. "Land Ho" became the first track on Side Two (the "Hard Rock Café" side) of *Morrison Hotel*, the Doors' fifth album, released the following February. Most critics would regard it as a successful rebound from their current offering, *The Soft Parade*, which had just been released after a frustrating nine months of work. In contrast, the first album had taken just six days to record. Like *Waiting For the Sun, Parade* suffered from a dearth of quality material, and Jim once again was in no mood—or condition—to work. It was also awash in strings and horns, an experiment that did not work. Elektra slapped a sticker on the cover boasting that it contained the hits "Touch Me," "Tell All the People," "Wishful Sinful" and "Running Blue," but only the first had been successful. The others were largely banned from the airwaves in the wake of the Miami debacle and didn't even make the Top 40. Nonetheless, the album eventually reached #6 on the charts and earned the band their fourth consecutive Gold Record Award.

Upon entering the workshop, there were several keyboards immediately to the left. Against the far left wall was Ray's Hammond B-3 organ, and in front of that, its keys also positioned parallel to the wall, was a new Farfisa organ. The model escapes me, but it was the same one I bought in Germany two years later, not realizing at the time that it was the model Ray had. At a right angle to the Farfisa was a Vox Continental with a Fender Rhodes key Bass sitting on top. The drums were situated beyond the keyboards, with John's back against the wall, a position common for him. The far end of the room was Robby's domain. When Jim was in attendance, he would stand roughly right of the room's center when he sang. And the strange, unnatural pattern I saw on the carpet my first day in the workshop? That, someone told me, was where Jim usually threw up…

One of Robby's bad habits was leaving his Gibson guitar lying on the floor, where it was inevitably stepped on and broken. Vince had to repair it several times. Only recently did I learn that the Gibson was stolen sometime in 2006. Robby had several guitars, including two acoustic models (I don't remember the manufacturer) in very large black hard shell cases. These were kept in the back storage area, next to the Acoustic amps. In concert, Robby used two guitars: the red Gibson Melody-maker and a black Gibson Les Paul with thicker gauge strings, used on numbers such as "Wild Child" or blues tunes. In the small compartment of the Les Paul case, near the neck, were two bottlenecks broken off of wine bottles. Robby didn't like to use a steel slide because it didn't give him the same pure sound as on "Moonlight Drive" and similar songs.

In concert, Robby used a one-and-a-half foot long effects bar made by Acoustic that featured several buttons for creating different sounds. I don't recall him having a wah-wah pedal, for which I was grateful. I hated wah-wah pedals. Still do. They are obnoxious!

Robby would tune up in the dressing room, usually with success. Sadly, at the second Isle of Wight Festival in September of 1970, his guitar was out of tune, no doubt one of the reasons—the other being Jim's somnambulant performance—very little of the Doors' set has ever been released. With Jim already sleep deprived, the band took the stage around two in the morning, playing in a cold wind for an audience more primed for the next act, the Who. The festival was the last major appearance by Jimi Hendrix, and to some it must have seemed as though it could have been Jim Morrison's swan song as well. I'm glad I wasn't there.

My job, basically, was to be able to take over for Vince if he was incapacitated. He had me learning the color codes for the guitar cord and cable lengths. Each cord had colored tape at either end to designate length. I learned how to make guitar cords and how to install the heat syncs on the back of each monolith amp. I was also able to hook up the two green metal transformers to the amps. Part of the gig was properly unpacking and packing all the equipment. Then it had to be moved. Vince had manuals about electronics, but I never had time to give them more than a glance. With the Doors it was always GO! GO! GO!

* * *

– 9 –

MEXICO

Forty years later, it is difficult to put everything in precise chronological order, but the most vivid memories of my time with the Doors occurred in Mexico City. Sometime toward the end of June I went upstairs to the Doors' office and saw a couple of Hispanic guys talking with Bill Siddons. As I was soon to learn, one of them was Javier Castro, a younger brother of dictator Fidel, and the other Mario Lomos, an interior decorator and concert promoter. Initially there had been negotiations for a Doors concert to be held at the Plaza Monumental, the largest bullring in Mexico City, but the Mexican government, apprehensive about what Jim's behavior might be, canceled the appearance. The scheduled date—June 28—was also the anniversary of a massive student demonstration the year before, and officials feared Jim might be tempted to provoke another. In its place, Castro offered a four night stand at his one-thousand seat nightclub The Forum, also located in Mexico City. Since the Doors continued to be regarded as lepers by most American concert promoters, Siddons booked the gig, which guaranteed the band $5,000 per-show. According to at least once account, the Doors were less than pleased when informed of the deal only after it had been signed, but Ray, Robby and John eventually decided to take their wives along and make it a working vacation. (Ray remembers the trip fondly. John does not.) Jim's fiery girlfriend, Pamela Courson, remained behind, which was probably what Jim preferred.

Also joining us for the trip was the late Jerry Hopkins, a reporter for Rolling Stone, who many years later would co-author *No One Here Gets Out Alive*, the first biography of Jim Morrison, and write its follow-up, *The Lizard King—The Essential Jim Morrison*. I never saw much of him after we landed in Mexico, except once in the dressing room.

The day before we left for Mexico, Vince and I collected the new road boxes for the monolith amplifiers, made at a seedy looking place that resembled the set of *Sanford & Son*. The next morning we headed for LAX in a rented red Chrysler cargo van. I sat in back, where there was no view whatsoever. Jim and Bill left at the same time in a sharp maroon BMW 2002, with Bill at the wheel. They shot ahead of us and were very quickly out of sight. Vince told me that they were taking a different flight than the rest of us. I couldn't help but think of how ignominious my position was—a "gofer" in every respect. And Bill Siddons always made sure I knew my place. He always seemed hollow to me, all sunglasses and bluster. Jim's puppet, as Vince said to me years later. A real "yes" man. My low opinion of Siddons was not going to change in Mexico.

At LAX, Vince and I began the regular process of funneling the twelve large, long coffins onto the plane as baggage. Vince gave the handler the usual huge tip to avoid airfreight charges, then we went upstairs to the boarding area. Everyone but Jim was milling around. Robby and I wanted a sandwich, so we walked into a nearby lounge and looked around. There were a couple dozen men in the place, all dressed in matching gray suits.

Robby, sporting a scraggly beard and fringed leather jacket, muttered, "I don't like this place. Let's get out of here."

In my infinite capacity for adolescent hyperbole, I remarked, "You look a lot like a friend of mine who lives back in Indiana." I was referring to Phil Kresler.

"He's the good looking one, right?"

"Yeah."

We never did get a sandwich, and before long the plane was open for boarding, the wives—Julia Densmore, Dorothy Manzarek, Lynn Krieger—walking ahead of each of their husbands. As many Doors fans are aware, Lynn had been one of Jim's earlier conquests, but she ended up with Robby, or maybe I should say she and Robby fell in love. I don't know if she was the woman who inspired Robby to compose "Hit Me," but he evidently had been a bad boy somewhere down the line. When he brought the tune to the studio, Jim said, "I'm not going to sing that." The title was changed to "Touch Me."

We took off late in the afternoon and veered out over the Pacific in our turn to the south. The plane was a 737, and I was amazed that it was large enough for all of the band's equipment. I sat next to Vince and had the window seat. We were in first class. During the flight, Ray, John and Robby passed around unremarkable photos taken on their recent vacation in Baja. There were no pictures of Jim, which was not surprising. Except for when they toured, Jim didn't hang around with the other three and had not gone to Baja. By 1969 the Doors were no longer as close as they had once been, particularly after Ray, John and Robby attempted to license "Light My Fire" for a car commercial without consulting Jim. They were associates more than "pals." Jim wasn't even pals with himself.

That evening, as we flew at cruising altitude, I watched a thunderstorm raging above the mountains, one of the most impressive weather events I have ever witnessed. Fortunately, we were well above it; riders on the storm roughly two years before the song was born. However, Jim was always in the midst of an emotional thunderstorm, regardless of where he found himself.

During our approach into Mexico City, some plumbing broke in the first class galley. A small wave washed down the aisle, and we were all standing on our seats as the plane touched down. A mobile staircase was hooked up, and though we were able to exit quickly, everyone came to a halt about half way down. There was a gaggle of reporters and photographers on the tarmac and, man, the flashes from the cameras came hot and heavy. I had never deplaned like that before, or since. At the bottom of the stairs, a microphone was jammed in my face, hitting me right in the mouth. We fought our way through the paparazzi and were seated in the VIP lounge. I sat next to Ray and Dorothy on one end of a black couch. Another microphone was thrust at me.

"Ray, what is your opinion of Richard Nixon?" the reporter asked me.

"I think Nixon will do his thing, man," I responded, "but I'm not Ray. That's Ray right there." I pointed to Ray, sitting to my left, one foot away.

The reporter moved on to Ray and Dorothy

After what seemed like half an hour, we got ready to be whisked to waiting cars. Several voices yelled, "Ready? Go!" and everyone ran into the large airport hallway. On our left, about two hundred yards away, were several girls who barely noticed us as we raced toward a limousine and a VW bug. Vince and I got into the VW with two women. I heard that one of them, Mario Lomos' girlfriend, was a porn star in Mexico. I don't remember her name, but I certainly remember her companion, Elizabeth. She was a sulky brunette who was very easy on the eyes. Her usual attire was a sheer, almost transparent lavender blouse. She obviously did not care for bras. I was to spend a lot of my time in Mexico City with Elizabeth.

The VW brought us to a very large cargo truck, where Bill Siddons and the equipment were waiting. The car whisked the women away, and we trucked the gear over to the Forum. It was already near ten o'clock and it took us about an hour to unload everything. We hit the road again and, around midnight, arrived at the Parque de los Principes, *Place of the Princes*, a semi-fancy motel set against a lush green hill and surrounded by palm trees and plenty of other vegetation. The place wasn't large, but it looked comfortable. There was a gated entrance, and beyond it, on the right, was a small guardhouse. A certain James Douglas Morrison was sitting resplendently on a wooden bench just inside the door. His leather pants and coat were dark chocolate, his blood red shirt straight out of 18th century France. He looked as if he could have been hanging out with Danton, leader of the French Revolution.

"Looks like you caught the wrong flight," I said.
"Yeah?"
"The press was everywhere," said Vince.
"Just my luck," Jim said.
"Grab those two guitars and take them up to Robby's room," Vince instructed me.

As I walked with the very large cases containing Robby's ornate flamenco guitars, Jim came up behind me and leaned close to my right ear. I could hear a grinding sound. I looked and saw a mischievous expression on his face. Even in the dim light I could see his bottom teeth and, wow, were they ever out of line! They were bent more at a forty-five degree angle than straight up and down, and he evidently was trying to impress me with the weird grating noise they could make. He also did this to Vince and Bill as we strolled to the large white two-story building at the rear of the villa.

"Have your ears popped yet?" Jim asked Vince.
"Yeah."
"Mine haven't, and we landed hours ago."
"Mine did, too," I said.
"Who gives a shit?" said the Lizard King.

"Now, now, boys," Bill chided.

We walked up the stairs on the left side of the building to the second floor, which was also the top floor. The Doors had reserved all ten rooms. No surprise. I roomed with Vince. Also no surprise. There were no towels, but we didn't care. We were beat, and crashed almost immediately. *Ist danken Gott*—thank God!—we had separate beds.

The next day, Vince and I returned to the Forum to set up, background music courtesy of the only album Vince had brought with him, the second by Blood, Sweat and Tears, which we played by wiring a turntable through the P.A.

The Forum was a huge Las Vegas style nightclub with a very large foyer, carpeted in red. The main room had terraced tables, and at the far end, opposite the stage, a balcony. Under the balcony was a long room where I discovered a grand piano, the maker of which I don't recall. Nor do I remember bothering to try it out. The dressing room was located upstairs from stage left. It was expansive and quite swank, its walls papered with an artistic black and white pattern. Above a long counter top and several chairs was a typical make-up mirror, and along one wall a large black leather couch. There always seemed to be two tall bottles of tequila on the coffee table. Several times I saw the same two security guards—attired in suits rather than uniforms—attempting to suck out and eat the worms floating in the booze!

Two other Mexican gentlemen, allegedly "friends of the band," made it clear that they were in possession of some magic mushrooms that we all could take later in the week. The band passed, as did Vince and I. We had more important things to do. In addition to setting up and testing the equipment, we stayed in contact via walkie talkies during every performance in case the balance of the sound had to be adjusted.

There wasn't much to do before the band showed up for the pre-show sound check except walk around the city, which is what Vince, Bill and I did that first day. Across the street from the Forum was a sidewalk concession selling various drinks, most of them fruity. And most of them smelling like a cesspool. Bill bought one anyway, and was struck by a wicked case of Montezuma's Revenge soon after. Someone told me that when Siddons went to use the first floor crapper, the porcelain throne backed up, soiling his pants and necessitating a long drive back to the villa for a fresh pair. Talk about instant karma. Couldn't have happened to a nicer fella… Truth be told, Montezuma would come for me later, and I literally wished someone would bring me a pistol. I felt that bad. On this occasion I wisely had a Coke. To my knowledge, the only band member laid low by intestinal south of the border demons was John Densmore. One morning I accompanied Julia on a mission to locate a pharmacy that could fill John's prescription.

On the front wall of the Forum was a huge hand-painted portrait of Jim, under which Ray posed for a now familiar photo. As we stood drinking and regarding the artwork, a pack of young boys approached us, repeatedly chattering, "Where is YEEM?" We pleaded ignorance.

Unlike the proposed bullring concert, which would have been priced so that virtually anyone could afford to attend, the Forum shows were for the more well-heeled crowd. I remember seeing a lot of young men sporting gold neck chains and flashy rings. They all seemed to drive Ford Mustangs. And their favorite number was definitely "The End," so popular in Mexico that Elektra had released it there as a single.

On one occasion, the son of President Diaz invited himself and a couple buddies into the dressing room, usually the scene of some pandemonium before a show. He was wearing a Nehru jacket and appeared to be stoned. He was also unwelcome, but the band made the best of the intrusion.

Unfortunately, another awkward dressing room incident happened to involve me. It was about an hour before the show, the Doors were sitting around, and Robby asked me to get his red Melody Maker. I handed the guitar to him and sat on the end of the couch nearest the door. Jim was talking to a couple of people, and as he talked he walked over and sat down next to me—smack diddly damn into the middle of a huge silver platter of deviled eggs. He immediately stood up, his leather pants now caked with yellow goo. I reached over and started wiping the mess off of his ass. BIG MISTAKE!

"WHAT THE HELL ARE YOU DOING?" he roared. "WHO NEEDS YOUR FUCKIN' ASS AROUND HERE ANYWAY? GET THE FUCK OUT!"

The other Doors looked at me as if to say: a.) We wouldn't help you in a million years. Or b.) Now you know what we've been putting up with.

"Okay, man," I said. "Whatever you want."

WOW…talk about being emotionally hammered. I went down to the stage area and had a Bohemia beer. Make that *another* Bohemia beer. The booze was free all week, compliments of Javier Castro. I was upset, but there was nothing I could do. I had just seen Jim Morrison at his worst, and it was ugly. As I look back now I understand how much pressure he was under, but that doesn't abrogate the fact that, when drinking, Jim became Jimbo, who was quite a PRICK.

Once onstage, his leather pants free of egg, Jimbo morphed back into Jim, charming the audience by introducing the band in Spanish: "Juan Densmore, Ramon Manzarek, Roberto Krieger, and me…Fidel Castro." The crowd exploded in uproarious laughter. They knew that whole Castro *thang*…

The following morning we all piled into a small bus—more accurately a very large van—and we went across town to the Anthropological Museum. Jim rode shotgun in the front seat. I was in the last seat in back, on the same side as Jim. Traffic in Mexico City circa 1969 was quite bad, and we were moving slow enough for a school bus filled with little girls to get a good look at us. One girl glanced down, and I could tell by the look of incredulity on her face that she recognized Jim. As the van passed, I gave her a rather unfriendly sneer. That was the Doors way—unfriendly. I was just trying to earn my stripes. However, looking back, I regret that I didn't smile or wave instead. So much so that I once started a tune called "Little Girl of Mexico." I either hated it, or at least didn't finish, which was the case with most of the music I composed.

There were about ten magnetic American girls walking around a huge pillar in the museum plaza. They were watching what looked like rain emanating from the ceiling, but when they saw Jim they became remoras suddenly drawn to a shark. He sat down on a bench in an adjacent area and chatted with the prettiest of them while the rest of us went on our way. John, Ray, Dorothy, Robby and Lynn continued through the museum.

Later, Vince, Bill, and I walked around the corner to a restaurant for a private open-air lunch beside massive light gray stone walls. We were joined by Luis, one of the two limousine chauffeurs who were at our disposal. Evidently he had followed the bus in case someone needed a ride. Jim was also there, with Julia Densmore. It wasn't long before several of the restaurant's female employees, pens in hand, came over to our table with albums for Jim to autograph. As we were being served, I noticed that Jim was being quite conciliatory towards Julia.

"Would you like to go back to the villa?" he asked her.
"No, not right now. But in a little while."
"Okay."

Decades later I learned from one of the many books about the Doors that Julia had come to Mexico to have a particular female surgery performed. I won't mention which.

"Bill," Vince said suddenly, "I need Luis to take Doug back to the Forum to start setting up for tonight."

"Luis," said Bill, "can you catch a taxi for the gringo?" Siddons obviously did not feel I was important enough to warrant a limousine ride.
"Si."

I followed Luis out to the busy, tree-lined street in front of the museum and waited in the shade while he tried to flag down a cab. No luck. I got my limo ride after all, sitting in the back in my serape and smoking a fat cigar. The windows of the black Caddy weren't tinted, so several cars were slowing down or speeding up, their occupants staring at me. *Who is that young gringo in the fancy car?* A rather heady experience for a snot-nosed seventeen-year-old.

About half an hour later, we arrived at the Forum. And guess what? Luis got out, slammed the door, and instead of opening my door, went inside the club. I tried the handle and discovered I was locked in. The other back door was also locked. So, ignominiously, I had to climb over the front seat and let myself out.

As the afternoon wore on I assembled, plugged in, turned on and generally put all of the instruments into performance readiness. While I was playing chords on Robby's Gibson, some of the club's waiters shouted at me because the noise was interrupting a bullfight they were watching on television. What a drag. Messing with that guitar and all those amps was FUNNN!

Ray was currently using a Gibson Kalamazoo organ and, as usual, a Fender Rhodes Key bass. The organ has a unique sound, reminding me of a Hoover vacuum cleaner except, of course, that each note is properly pitched. In other words, it makes a spooky sound. And when the Doors combined this sound with Robby's feedback and modal solos, and Jim's baritone vocals, it was truly an eerie sound. A *new* sound. Aside from John's jazz influences, I really liked the way he tuned his drums…LOW. It gave the band's sound a menacing bottom, like THUNDER. I remember a rehearsal at 8512 Santa Monica Boulevard when Ray hit a low D on the key bass and made the sticks laid across John's floor tom dance. The drum was obviously also tuned to a low D. It's all about the VIBRATIONS, isn't it?

When the Doors showed up, I brought the Gibson to the dressing room and handed it to Robby. While Vince checked to make sure I'd done everything correctly, members of the opening act filed in, roughly thirteen Mexican musicians in black suits and white shirts. They had a brass section and all of the standard instruments. The guitarist had some effects device that sounded like a police siren, and when they played certain songs he used that siren too damn much. Give me a break! I asked a couple of these guys if one night I could sit in with them to play "Light My Fire," one of many Doors numbers I knew note for note, and they responded in the affirmative.

After the Mexican group finished their set, the Doors took the stage, their entrance not quite as dramatic in a club as in a large hall. However, the performance was more intimate, with Jim singing to the people who sat sucking on drinks at linen covered tables only a few feet from the stage. The place was packed. Everyone wanted to hear "Fidel and the Boys."

The Doors didn't agree on a set list easily. Many were the times Ray and John would start one tune, and Robby would start another. Robby usually won. As quiet as he is, he is also very strong willed on stage. I specifically recall a time that Ray and John launched into "Light My Fire" as Robby began "Love Me Two Times." Within a few seconds, the chaos ended and everyone was playing "Love me Two Times."

One afternoon, the band and their significant others went to check out some Aztec ruins. I was invited, and now wish I'd gone. But I stayed behind to buy gifts for Kathy and my family, not knowing if I'd get another opportunity. Bill was still at the villa, so I asked him if he wanted to share a cab to the recommended shopping area. He declined, claiming he had work to do. I grabbed a cab alone.

Who did I see in the very first store I entered? GODDAMN BILL SIDDONS! What a lying sack of horseshit… He said he was looking for a shirt for Jim, and asked me if I wanted to grab lunch, as if he hadn't done anything wrong, so we went to a nearby restaurant. We didn't say much…

– 10 –

MY SWIM WITH JIM

After the concert the entire Doors entourage ended up back at the Parque de los Principes, only to have someone suggest returning to the city for some club hopping. I asked Bill if I could go along. To his eternal credit, he said, "Sure." Luis brought the limo around. Jim jumped in the back, sitting between Frank Lisciandro and Bill, and I rode shotgun in the front. The five of us were going to PARTAY!

Our first stop was some insipid dance hall that looked dead, almost no one there. I didn't understand why we bothered. We left immediately and went to a taco stand, where we ingested some authentic grub.

"I can feel those tacos creepin' out my asshole," Jim remarked. I'm sure that Mexican food had a similar effect on all of us.

The next stop was sure to be a winner: Sergio's de Club. This place seemed more promising—palm trees on either side of the sidewalk, and large oak front doors with Spanish style handles. It was dark inside, carpeted and comfortable, with a loft running all around the room. As soon as we walked in, "Hello, I Love You" blasted from the sound system. Instantly, both Jim and Bill shouted, "Take that OFF!"

I asked one of the waiters where the turntable was, and he pointed toward the loft. I went up there, took the Doors record off and slapped on Iron Butterfly's "Inna Gadda Da Vida." When I went back down, the guys were already seated at a table, Jim with his back to the wall. I sat next to him. He looked up as if searching for a planet in the night sky, just above the horizon, and ran the end of his right little finger along the edge of his moustache. "Iron Butterfly," he muttered softly, as though making some announcement to the dream world.

Sergio, the club's owner, had gray hair and moustache, elegant sideburns and was dressed in stylishly cut Spanish clothing. He came over and asked Jim to say hello to some people at a nearby table. Jim agreed and followed him, but they weren't gone long. When the glad handing was over, Sergio and Jim returned to our table. Sergio asked, "What are you drinking?"

"I'll have a Morrison special," said Jim.
"What's that?" Sergio asked.
"Rum and Coke. Heavy on the rum."

"And you?" Sergio asked me.

"A Morrison special."

With the drinks came cigars, none but the finest: Monte Cruz Las Palmas. Jim bit off the end of one, fired that bad boy up, and proceeded to smoke luxuriously. Frank also lit one, then began chatting to Jim about the film *Feast of Friends*, a Doors documentary Frank had made with Paul Ferrara, another of Jim's friends from the UCLA days. The previous month, *Feast of Friends* had won first prize in the documentary division at the Atlanta International Film Festival. There was also some talk about possibly doing a gig with Iron Butterfly. Jim excused himself to go to the shithouse, and I followed.

"Man," I said, "you sure do have a cool middle name…Douglas. That's my middle name, Bruce Douglas Cameron. James Douglas Morrison…"

"Why don't you shut up and get drunk, all right?"

After we left the club, I was walking behind Jim when we came upon a woman standing to the right of the sidewalk, holding a small child. She was begging. Jim gave her a five dollar bill. That would have been about fifty bucks in pesos.

We jumped back into the limo and were back at the villa by three in the morning. In Frank's room, Jim told us a joke about a guy with a harelip telling a hunchbacked bartender that the drink prices are too high. His imitation of a harelip was actually quite good.

"The bartender finally says, You know, I have to thank you for not mentioning my affliction."

"What affliction? the harelip asks."

"My hunchback."

"Hunchback, hell! Everything's so high in here, I thought it was your ass!"

Just as Jim got to the punch line, deep snoring emanated from Frank, who was out cold.

"Well, it wasn't that funny," Jim said.

"Ha!" Siddons laughed.

I had heard the exact same joke from a cat in high school named Mark Place, but I chuckled anyway. At the same time, I felt like I was in a dream. There I was, standing in a Mexican villa at three in the morning, listening to Jim Morrison telling jokes.

"Okay," I said, "I've got one for you. There's this Swede named Sven who goes into the forest with two friends to do some hunting. He says, 'Now, listen—we'll split up and meet back here on this spot in two hours. If you get lost, just shoot. Then we can find ya.' All three go off on separate trails. The two hour deadline comes and goes, and Sven's buddies meet as planned. No Sven. Several hours go by. Finally, Sven comes plodding out of the forest. 'Why didn't you shoot?' his friends ask. 'I did,' says Sven, 'but I ran out of arrows.'"

"Ya got any more good ones?" Jim asked.

"Ha-ha, no…"
"Brilliant," said Siddons.

We walked over to the adjoining room with Jim, and he told us another joke, one about a guy and his wife in New York. I don't remember the joke.

"I'm going to bed," Bill said.
"No one's going to go swimming?" I asked.
"I am," Jim replied.
"Me, too," I said. "I'll see you at the pool in a couple."
"Yep," said the Lizard King.

I went to my room, where Vince was asleep, and discovered there were no towels. I bopped down to the right end of the upper hallway just as Jim, in his swim suit and carrying a towel, came out of his room.

"Hey, Jim, could you grab me an extra towel? There were none in our room."
"Sure."

He grabbed a towel from his room and handed it to me. We went down two flights of stairs and walked a few steps to the medium sized oval-shaped pool. It was surrounded by lawn, with a few tables and several chaise lounge chairs here and there. At the deep end of the pool was a small diving board, and the only lights were those glowing underwater.

Jim dove in first. I stripped down to my very suave jockey shorts and jumped into the shallow end. The water felt great and sobered me up a bit, even though neither of us was by any means drunk. As Jim swam up and down the length of the pool several times, I stood against the right wall in the shallow end and looked around. In the darkness, to the right of the villa, I could just make out a series of small cottages that housed the rich American tourists I had seen earlier in the day. Jim swam over to me.

"You know, Vince and I did a sound rental gig with your P.A. last week," I said. "It was at the Santa Monica Civic Auditorium with that band Sweetwater."

"A nice hall," said Jim. "We've played there."
"I met this really foxy Asian chick at that gig. When I mentioned the Doors, she said, 'Oh, I used to go out with Jim.' Do you remember her name?"

Jim immediately plunged back under the water and swam down to the deep end. Right away I realized: 1.) I've put my foot in my mouth again. 2.) Jim usually doesn't care to talk about the past. But I learned that there *were* exceptions to rule number two.

As Jim climbed up the ladder in the deep end to use the diving board, his hair trailing halfway down his back, he said, "I really dig the chlorine. It's very good for your hair."
"I guess," I said. "Did you swim in high school?"
"Yeah, did you?"

"Junior high and high school. Six years, and summers at the Jewish Community Center."

"Jewish Community Center?"

"Yeah. You could join even if you weren't Jewish. We swam against country club teams."

"Umm," Jim murmured. "What events?"

"Started out with some backstroke and 'fly,' but my strength was always the sprints, fifty yard and one hundred yard freestyle."

"The same," said Jim. "That's what I swam."

"Well, with a sprint, you better have a damn good racing start," I said. "When I hit the water I made sure I hit it hard so I didn't submerge too much."

Jim smiled briefly. "So, let's see what ya got."

I climbed up the ladder in the shallow end, turned to my left, and then faced left again. I stood facing the shallow end, about one foot from the edge.

"Swimmers to your mark," said Jim. I took one step and was now standing right at the edge. "Take your mark," Jim added.

As all competitive swimmers know to do, I simultaneously curled my toes to grip the edge of the pool with my feet while I crunched down to be ready to spring forward.

"GO!" the Lizard King shouted.

I launched myself through the air and smacked smartly on the water in a racing start that even ol' Montezuma himself would have admired.

Then we reversed the process, with me as starter and Jim the swimmer. I was standing about mid-pool, half bobbing because it was deeper, and when I yelled "Go!" I was presented with a snapshot moment that I'll never forget if I live to be one hundred. Jim Morrison, his arms outstretched, wild hair and beard—and even wilder eyes—flying through the air like the ancient mariner jumping ship.

We laughed it up a bit. I felt somewhat uncomfortable in essentially a wet pair of underwear, but I got over it. We swam around idly for a few minutes, not saying much, and eventually stopped at the deep end. I was hanging from the diving board while Jim clutched the ladder.

"So, Jim, what are you going to do when you're done with the Doors?" I asked.

There was a long pause. "I'd like to start a nightclub."

"A nightclub?"

"Yeah."

"Called what?"

Another long pause. "The Albatross."

"Water, water everywhere, nor any drop to drink," I remarked.

"The Rime of the Ancient Mariner," said Jim.

"Who wrote that?"

"Samuel Coleridge."

"I really enjoyed reading that poem. It's a metaphor, isn't it?"

"What do you know about metaphors?" Professor Morrison asked. "Talk to me."

"I know about metaphors," I insisted. "Like the river in *Huckleberry Finn*. It's a metaphor for life. Or the Doors. For me, you guys are like a metaphor for Eternity. 'Break On Through.' Right?"

"Um-hmm. Eternity."

"But," I continued, "my favorite metaphor is from *Moby Dick*, when Captain Ahab says to Starbuck, 'You and I were here a million years before this sea rolled.' Or words to that effect. That really gets to me. It's the Doors of Perception thing…when the doors of perception are cleansed. The sea in *Moby Dick* is a metaphor for eternity."

"A-plus," said Jim.

"*Moby Dick* and *Huck Finn*—those two compete for the greatest American novel ever written. At least that's what Mrs. Chamberlain said."

"Who's that?"

"My English teacher at West High."

"Oh."

Jim submerged and swam all the way down to the shallow end without coming up for air. As I watched him go, I couldn't help but feel that maybe now he viewed me as being at least slightly more intellectual than the average screaming Doors nut.

"I'll bet you five bucks I can swim farther underwater than you," I shouted as he surfaced.

After a moment of thought, he shook his head. "Nah…why should I kill myself for five bucks?"

I remembered that Jim and Bill had a contest going to see who could quit smoking. Jim would walk up to Bill if Bill had a cigarette, grab one of his elbows and punch him hard on the bicep. I tried joining in once, slugging Jim's arm when I caught him smoking at the villa. But he yanked his arm away and said, "You weren't in on it."

"Oh, right," I agreed. Hopefully Jim would remember me more for our discussion of literature.

By the time we grabbed our towels and headed back to the villa, the dim light of dawn was just beginning to overtake the nighttime gloom.

"Goodnight, Jim," was all I could think of to say.

"Night, man."

As I walked down the open aisle to my wonderful room with Vince, I could hear Jim's door close behind me. A very memorable night, no doubt. Sometimes it seems so surreal that I wonder if it really happened. But, of course, it did.

– 11 –

ELIZABETH

Whenever the Doors performed, Vince and I obviously had to be there. In Mexico, we usually had a bit of free time early in the evening, though I'd occasionally be assigned some sort of "gofer" task. I usually did these chores with a minimum of grumbling, but one night's assignment was a gas, no reason for grumbling whatsoever. Mario Lomos showed up in the dressing room, Elizabeth on his arm and looking just as gorgeous as when I'd first met her at the airport. Mario asked if I'd mind going with her to his house to retrieve some specially framed photographs of Jim. I hoped my shit eating grin wasn't too obvious.

The next thing I knew, Elizabeth and I were gliding through downtown Mexico City in her red AMC Javelin. I noticed that the speedometer was metric. And at Mario's house I noticed that what Jim wore in the photos was the white Mexican wedding shirt Bill Siddons had bought for him the day Bill declined to share a taxi with me. Jim would wear that shirt the following month when the band played the Aquarius Theatre in Hollywood. Elizabeth rummaged around for something else—maybe pills for Mario—and then sat next to me on the couch. The lights were low, and I was feeling more than a little fine. Life sure did flow at a pleasant pace in Mexico City. But I was definitely in no mood to take a siesta! Elizabeth was wearing a sheer lavender blouse, possibly the same one she had on at the airport. And she still had not found a brassiere. Her long dark hair was the color of a raven's wing. We kissed a couple of times, and I became even more acutely aware of her charms. Unfortunately, we had to leave, but as a consolation prize she let me drive back to the Forum. I felt as if I were riding a rocket through the upper stratosphere.

When we arrived at the Forum, my adrenaline rush was destined to continue. Elizabeth followed me backstage, where I quickly assured myself that the Doors' equipment was ready to go. The opening act, already in mid-set, finished what they had been playing. I stood next to Ray's organ, looked at the drummer and said, "'Light My Fire?'" He nodded. I turned to the bass player, who was standing on the drum riser, and asked, "Do you mind if I play bass?"

Without waiting for an answer, I yanked the guitar cord out of his bass and jammed it into Ray's Fender Rhodes Key Bass. This was going to be UNBELIEVEABLE!! I sat down, put my right foot on the volume pedal, stomped it much closer to FULL TILT BOOGIE, played a couple of notes on the Gibson to make sure, then looked at the drummer. "Hit it!"

BANG! The snare shot crashed through the Forum. Then the organ riff ran through the cycle of fifths, a Hoover vacuum suddenly transformed into an orchestra. The progression shifted from major to minor, from straight 4/4 to a Latin style, and a seventeen-year-old kid sang, "You know that it would be untrue / You know that I would be a liar…"

A thousand people let out a cheer, and the next ten minutes were, needless to say, unforgettable. I played the song note for note, as I'd learned it from the record. I suspect I'm the only "band boy"—as Vince called us—who ever got to play "Light My Fire" through the Doors' sound system. I was impressed by how well the band knew the tune. Then again, didn't everybody? With that, the set was over, and the band slowly packed up their gear and left the stage.

Vince cornered me. "What do you mean by playing that song? That's the Doors' encore!"
"Er, I think they liked it," I said.
"Well, don't do THAT again!"
"I'll go get Robby's guitar."
"Yeah, you do that."

Vince instructed me to take the walkie-talkie out to the cloak room under the balcony and check the sound balance. I don't remember much about the show except that the Doors were good.

I found Elizabeth in the dressing room after the concert. Although she spoke almost no English and I no Spanish, we were able to communicate. As I got to know her better, I was more and more mesmerized by her beauty. She kept telling me, "I need protection." I told Vince I would be leaving with Elizabeth, and though he was definitely nonplussed, he didn't say much.

It was around midnight as she and I pulled up to her apartment building. The wrought iron gate swung open, and a security guard motioned us to drive through. He gave us a knowing look as we left the car and went up to her place.

Elizabeth had a nice apartment, and within a few minutes it was filled with the sound of the Doors' first album. In short order she broke out a pipe and some hemp. I could not have cared less about the hemp, which she managed to spill all over her bed. I brushed it off the sheets, and she said something in Spanish that didn't sound very happy. I kissed her, and one thing led to another. It goes without saying that I experienced a wonderful evening. I felt quite worldly. And very happy.

We awoke early, and Elizabeth gave me a ride back to the villa. When Bill saw me, he made a couple of cracks, one of which was, "Oh, the wandering minstrel has come back into the fold."

* * *

– 12 –

THE END

I don't remember much about the Doors' final performance in Mexico City, but a few weird things happened after the gig. There were two streets running parallel on either side of the Forum, and twenty or thirty steps to the left of the club entrance was a lot of traffic. To the right, in about twice as many steps, was a quieter backstreet, which was where the equipment van sat. The limousine was double-parked and running, Luis at the wheel. I stood with Jim and Bill at the open right rear door. It must have been close to one in the morning. Jim was really lit up, repeatedly shouting, "Amigos—las revoluciones!" More and more people started gathering around, so Bill shoved him into the limo and jumped in behind. The door slammed shut, and Luis took off.

A few seconds later, a kid ran in front of a car coming from the other direction. BOOM! The car hit the kid, who rolled over and over about five times in the street and immediately stood up. The driver slammed on the brakes and got out. He was probably in his late twenties or early thirties, and I recognized him as the trumpet player for the opening act that had allowed me to perform "Light My Fire." He went over to the kid, who was now standing on the other side of the road. They spoke briefly, then the trumpet player simply got back behind the wheel and drove off. Apparently hitting a pedestrian in Mexico City in 1969 was no big deal if the victim could walk away.

The next morning—Sunday, June 29—Jim, dressed in his medium brown suede leathers and Frye boots, stood on the very wide cobbled sidewalk in front of the Parque de los Principes, waiting for the limo to take him to the airport. Vince glanced at him and said exactly what I was thinking: "Man, you've got a lot of grey hair on top, Mr. Morrison. I should be the grey one."

"Must be an occupational hazard," Jim replied.

The incident reminded me of a day earlier in the week when Jim, Bill and I were sitting in a little cantina across from the villa's guard shack. I sat across from Jim, only two feet away, and noticed that his teeth were as yellow as legal paper. To myself I wondered, *How much booze, drugs and cigarette smoke has gone down that gullet?* Jim was definitely "taking it hard on the boulevard."

By noon, the Doors and their entourage were on their way back to Los Angeles. All except Bruce Douglas Cameron and Vincent Treanor III. There I was, stuck in Mexico with Vince. What a mess. Vince said he would like to stay there with me for two weeks and look at pipe organs in the old cathedrals. The thought made me nauseous. No way. I was determined to remain resolute.

Elizabeth came by early that evening, and we drove away to make out in her car rather than the apartment. Around midnight we pulled up in front of the villa, and I told her, "Wait here." I went up to the room to find Vince.

"You were driving her car?" he asked.
"Yes."
"If you'd been in a wreck, they would have thrown you in jail. You don't have a Mexican driver's license. It would have been a long time before any of us saw you again."

The guard called up to the room and said I'd have to move the car, which was blocking the drive. Elizabeth couldn't do it because I had the keys. I told him I'd be right down, but Vince continued to lecture me. The phone rang again, and I ran downstairs to discover an American couple trying to drive through the gate. The woman was drunk and yelling obscenities. *Why couldn't you rich assholes walk forty yards to your bungalow and have the guard park your car?* I thought. Elizabeth was pretty upset, too. I moved the car, we traded seats and said our goodbyes. I don't remember trading addresses.

I returned to the room, fell into bed, but couldn't sleep. One thought kept nagging at me: *I've got to get out of here!*

About five in the morning I told Vince, "I'm quitting the band, man. If I'm not where the Doors are, that doesn't work for me. Give me my visa and passport." I called a cab.

"You'll never get through customs," said Vince.
"Goodbye." That's all I said before walking out the door, suitcase in hand.

The taxi was waiting, and I hopped in hoping I had enough cash for the fare. The ride took nearly half an hour, giving me more than enough time to verify that I indeed could pay my way. Barely…

At the Western Airlines departure area, I got in line with the other passengers and set my suitcase down.

"Passport, please," the ticket clerk said.
"Okay."
"Ticket, please."
I handed that over.
"And your visa, please."

I opened the visa and, to my amazement, what did I see? A document with the name Vincent Treanor III, age 33, not Doug Cameron, age 17. The old switcheroo. Thank you so much, Vince. The Prince of Deviousness had struck again.

The ticket agent looked at me quizzically. I thought, *Oh, great—now I'm up shit creek.*

I looked around, and right behind me I saw a familiar face: Bill Belmont, manager of Country Joe and the Fish. The Doors had hired him because they needed a translator who was fluent in Spanish. I was relieved, to say the least.

"Hey, Bill, how ya doin'?" I asked nervously.
"What are you on, Doug?"
"Nothing, man. Vince switched my visa on me, and now I have a problem here."

Bill walked around the edge of the counter and introduced himself to the agent. There was a mild exchange in Spanish, and in a very short time everything was smooth. I was checked through, followed by Bill.

"Would you like to have some breakfast?" he asked.
"Well, Bill, I'm a little low on cash."
"Piss on it. Come on. I'm meeting my dad for breakfast. You can join us."

The three of us ate a leisurely meal, and then it was plane time. Back to California, where I didn't know exactly what to expect now that I'd decided to quit. Bill and I sat together, and before we landed in Los Angeles, he leaned over to me.

"Here, man," he said. "Take two hundred pesos and convert them at LAX. You need a little cash. I'm catching another plane to San Francisco, but I'll settle it with Siddons later."

"Mr. Belmont," I said before we parted ways at the airport, "thank you *so, so* much. I don't know what I would have done without you."

"You're welcome, kid. Good luck." He turned and hurried away.

I owe Bill Belmont a huge debt of gratitude. I don't know if he's still alive, but he certainly exemplified the "peace and love" vibes that must have still been floating around San Francisco two years after the storied Summer of Love. He really was a lovely guy. Again, Bill, I owe you. Maybe I should have worked for Country Joe and the Fish. They performed at Woodstock less than two months later. The Doors did not.

Okay…I was feeling better now. I was back in L.A. I flagged down a cab and told the driver to take me to Vince's place on Durand Drive. By the time I found the hidden key and let myself in, it was close to three in the afternoon. BOOM…I crashed for a sorely needed nap. The fire was starting to burn itself out.

I awoke a few hours later, hungry as hell. As usual, there wasn't a scrap of food in the apartment. With only ten dollars left, I walked down through the hills to a grocery store on Franklin Avenue. It was a LONG walk. I bought the customary bill of fare that made up my diet in those days: A half-gallon of whole milk, a quart of chocolate milk and a box of powdered donuts. Outside the store, with the traffic whizzing by, I took a couple long slugs of the chocolate milk. *AHHH, that was better!* I didn't care who saw me or what they thought.

I walked down Franklin and cut over to Bronson Avenue, passing a number of small stores. Instead of giving in to the urge to inhale a few donuts, I went into a bookstore and browsed my way toward the back. A minute later, just as I turned and looked to the front of the store, in came James Douglas Morrison and Pamela Courson. I was stunned. Los Angeles is the proverbial sprawling metropolis—fifty-eight smaller cities jammed together and collectively called L.A. What were the chances I would bump into Jim and Pam? There are no accidents. At least this wasn't one. The divine powers had given me the final scene of my play.

"Doug…" Jim said warmly.
"Hi, Jim," I said incredulously. We shook hands.
"I'd like you to meet my girl, Pam."

She was about five foot eight, had apricot colored hair and wore standard hippie garb. My grocery sack of haute cuisine was cradled in my right arm, and I shifted it to my left so I could shake her hand.

"Oh, don't bother," she said, more than a little dismissively, and shuffled to the back of the store. She was just as self-centered as Jim, only not as friendly. No—she sure couldn't be bothered with me.

Jim and I stood there looking at each other as if we had been beamed down to the surface of Mars.

"What a strange coincidence," he said. He did that familiar bit of stroking the right side of his moustache with the little finger of his right hand.
"No shit," I replied.
"Where's Vince?"
"Still in Mexico."
"Where's the equipment?"
"Still in Mexico."
"How come you're up here, and he's down there?"
I took a deep breath. "Well, as I told you before, I've been having trouble with Vince. The cat is not heterosexual. He's been coming on to me. I don't work for him. I work for the Doors. You came back to L.A., so I came back to L.A."
" I see…Uh, did you get those pictures from Mario?"
"Nope. I saw them at his house, but that was before you said you wanted them. I never could get back there."
"How about the tapes I asked for? Did you do that?"
"How was I supposed to do that? Jim, I have almost no money. I haven't been paid by anybody."
"Oh, well, forget it," he said, obviously not wanting to help with my cash flow problem. "So, what are you doing now?"
"I'm staying up at Vince's, way up in the Hills. I had to walk down here to get something to eat."
"Yeah, we just came in to look at books."
"Small world."

"Yeah, isn't it? Well, we'll see you at the workshop Monday."

He had started walking towards Pam as he spoke, and I headed for the door. As we looked at each other for the last time, I said, "Yeah."

Two years later, almost to the day of our last meeting, Jim died.

I knocked down a few donuts as I made the long walk uphill to Vince's place. I had plenty of time to mull over the events of the previous sixteen days. My basic feeling was, *I just want to get the hell out of here! Get back home, to the Midwest…to Kathy.*

I called Dad and told him I had quit the Doors. He booked a flight home for me, then called our family friend Jeanne Battaglia. She hailed from Rockford, but was living in Los Angeles and was the personal assistant to Susan St. James, who was also a former native of Rockford and a couple years away from starring with Rock Hudson on the *McMillan & Wife* series. Jeanne picked me up from Durand Drive the next day, and we stopped at Susan's pad in Laurel Canyon before going to LAX. Susie was not home, but I was destined to see her again several years later. I had seen her in Rockford when she and I were both younger.

By the time Jeanne dropped me off at a hotel next to the airport, ticket and flight information in hand, it was mid-afternoon. She had truly come through in the clutch. If I'd ever had a big sister, it would have been Jeanne. We are still close to this day. I thanked her emphatically.

"Good luck, Dougger," she said. And drove away…

I arrived back in Indiana on Tuesday night. Dad and my Culver buddy, Phil Kresler, met me in Indianapolis. They had driven to the airport separately from different locations because Dad and I were leaving in the morning for two weeks of sightseeing across the West.

We spent the night at Phil's folks' place in Kentland, and on the ride there I couldn't help but wonder what the Doors might have said—if anything—when I didn't show up on Monday. I was more curious than anything. I didn't really care. I was HOME. Still, looking out the car window at the black Indiana night, I thought: *Damn, it's only July 2nd. And it's already over. The dream is over…*

As Phil and I were driving north on Highway 41 in his father's Corvette, with Dad bringing up the rear in a new white 1969 351 Mustang, someone in England looked at the bottom of a swimming pool and saw the lifeless body of Brian Jones.

* * *

Doug back home in Rockford after first summer at Culver '66.

Culver Black Horse Troop B – summer 1966

Doug just before the Holocaust performed on November 3, 1968. Thousands of faces behind him.

Doug Cameron meets Ray Manzarek, 11-03-68

Ray on the way to the stage. 11-03-68

Foreground – Steve Connell, Jim Morrison in trailer, 11-03-68

Doug Cameron standing, John Densmore sitting, 11-03-68

Ray and Robby ready to go on in Chicago – November 3, 1968

Doug and Kathy, Fall '69

Doug back in Rockford, two weeks after the Doors – July '69

Doug rockin' hard with Terra Firma in Mettendorf, Germany, 1972.

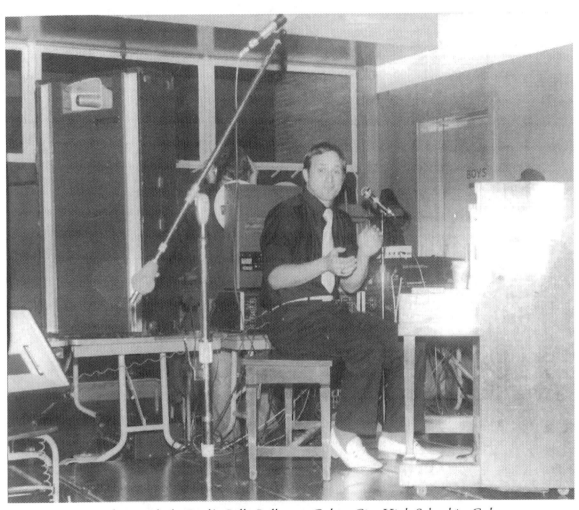

In mid set with the Rock'a Billy Rollers at Culver City High School in Culver City, California (January 5, 1979) during "That's Alright Mama."

At Ray's place on Ledgewood Drive in the Hollywood Hills, (April 1979)

On the strip, summer 2008

More radio and press interviews – Lafayette, Indiana (1991)

Doug with Jim Short at Culver, summer of 67. I had just heard Light My Fire the previous week.

That's Vince wearing the shiny shirt in Chicago, pre show set-up on June 14, 1969.

A view of the Doors from the wings, June 14, 1969 in Chicago.

Julia Densmore in Mexico City, with Bill.

Ray and John leave the stage after the final encore, June 14, 1969 at the Auditorium Theatre in Chicago.

Jim with all of the remoras at the Anthropology Museum in Mexico City

Bill Siddons and Mario Lomos at Parque de los Principes in Mexico City.

David Wallin and Doug at the Palomino Club in San Fernando Valley, Spring 1979.

Doug and the Rockabilly Rollers meet Buddy Holly's last bass player (Waylon Jennings) at the Palomino Club in the San Fernando Valley-February, 1979

David Letterman, Doug Cameron, and Robin Williams at the Comedy Store in Los Angeles, 1979.

Upstairs at the Doors workshop (now a bar) (Summer 2008)

PART TWO
AFTER THE FIRE

– 13 –

"MAYBE FIND IT BACK IN L.A...."

I felt a great wave of relief walking out of Indiana University's Assembly Hall with at least seven thousand other graduates on May 5, 1978. There is much to say about the life of Doug Cameron between 1969 and 1978, years that included a stint in the United States Air Force (12-28-69 to 04-20-72). Note that I still remember the exact dates. It would be safe to say that I hated every second I spent in the service, and I had enlisted, knowing that Vietnam was a possibility. I was a right brained person in an extremely left brained environment. Less than six months before, I was on a wild rollercoaster ride with the Doors; now I was a regimented servant of Uncle Sam. What would Jim Morrison have thought?

On the other side of the coin, I have to admit that I loved seeing as much of Germany as I did. Most of those German tales are for another book, but in looking back I am reminded of a topic I want to talk about: drugs. I am a Baby Boomer, a person who came of age in the late Sixties, and part of that turbulent scene was drugs. I *hate* drugs, both the illegal and so-called "recreational" varieties. Fortunately, I do not have an addictive personality. I know many people who do, and some of them are dead now. Drugs, thank God, scared me from the start. But they didn't scare me enough. While the list of drugs I never touched is long, there was one over-the-counter preparation available in Germany that I wish I'd never tried. They were typically marketed as diet pills, and perfectly legal. Technically, however, they were a form of speed, twenty pills in small glass containers. And they were horrible. A lot of servicemen popped them for extra energy and to help them stay awake on guard duty. One variety, Rosimon Neu, had a red label, and the label on the other, Rosimon Blau, was blue. I don't recall if the dosages were the same, but in short order a couple of those pills would have me buzzin' like a bee. If I took a couple every few hours, I'd stay high for a long time. Naturally, there had to be a downside, and that came when the effect of the pills wore off. However high I'd been, I would usually descend to a place lower than before taking the pills. They were probably the same uppers Elvis used while stationed in Germany, and everyone knows what happened to him. No thanks…

The standard term of enlistment for the Air Force is four years, and as the above dates indicate, I served far less than that. At the time I was discharged, there was a new program called "39-12." Maybe that isn't its official title, but 39-12 is the name of the regulation that allowed me to ultimately be defined as a person who could—and *should*—be discharged early. In other words, it was a program designed especially for military personnel who hated the service. It's a long, grueling story to which the reader will not be subjected. However, I want to stress that I at first received a General discharge under honorable conditions. Marvin Gaye was proud of his

General discharge. I was not. Six years later, as I prepared to graduate from Indiana University, I applied for an upgrade of my General discharge. Six Air Force officers at the Pentagon read my letter, and all but one voted for the upgrade. The Honorable discharge made me feel better because I had felt very guilty about not finishing my hitch. My dad fought in World War Two, as did his brothers Lew and George. After 1978, as the years rolled by, it gradually dawned on me how much the first discharge had bothered me. But time does have a way of healing all wounds. Most of them, anyway…

In the midst of the Guilt Years—1972 to 1978—I chose to adopt Indiana as my home state. I wanted to study piano at Indiana University, and my parents had moved from Rockford, Illinois, back to their hometown of Kokomo, Indiana, in 1970.

On December 13, 1972, the greatest musical day of my life unfolded. In front of a jury of musical directors from each regional campus of Indiana University, I played four compositions; classic literature from Bach to Prokofiev, and including a Clementi Sonata as well as a Waltz (Valse) by Chopin. I really wasn't very nervous before my performance. There was no time to be nervous. I spent nearly every waking hour playing piano in a little practice room at I.U. Kokomo. At the beginning of the fall semester I had made a daily practice chart and vowed to stick to it. I did. Now I had made it into P 300, which meant I was now a formal piano student at Indiana University!

During this time I befriended the weatherman at WLWI/Channel 13 in Indianapolis. His name? David Letterman. Yes, *that* David Letterman. We were by no means chums, just acquaintances. I had seen him in the spots he did for Bob Catterson Buick, sponsor of "Freeze Dried Movies" on Friday night. After each commercial, Dave would be shown sitting behind a desk. The film might be *Thunder Road*, but he would announce, "And now back to *When Godzilla Ate Detroit*, starring Don Rickles as the monster." Then someone off camera would throw something at Letterman. It was slapstick, and as one who loves the Three Stooges, I found it truly hilarious. I laughed so hard I cried, to employ an unavoidable cliché.

I was in a band at this time, and one day Dave asked me if we would play on his Saturday kids' show, *Clover Power*. Sure, I said. Any exposure was good exposure. The band was a collection of vagabond musicians from Kokomo called Sneed Hern, a moniker created by W.C. Fields in an old film. When he introduced us, Dave said, "Well, if you were planning on naming your next daughter Sneed Hern, forget it, because that name is already taken by a great band from Kokomo, Indiana, and they are here today."

The performance went well, but because I am so ANALLY RETENTIVE, I reached over and turned my Leslie 122 speaker down to almost zero before we got our cue from the director. Why I did this escapes me. The band sounded good, but no one could hear me. This was but one incident in a series of screw-ups that occurred during my long, serious quest for rock and roll stardom. That, however, is another book. This book is about my days with a band who *didn't* suffer from a lack of attention.

As for that band, I was sharply reminded of them one day in July of 1971, maybe around the tenth. I was in Germany, walking with some other G.I.s to the Gasthaus in the tiny Eifel mountain village of Weissmansdorf, when I heard the troubling news about Jim Morrison that I and many others inside the fire had come to fear.

One of my fellow airmen, a tall, bespectacled guy named Frank came up to me and said, "Man, Doug…did you hear the news about Jim Morrison?"

"No," I replied, expecting the worst.
"He died."
"What?"
"He died," said Don Impink. "In Paris. About a week ago."

I was already quite unhappy with my lot in life, and the news of Jim's death certainly didn't do anything to improve the situation. At first I didn't want to believe it, but as the days went by it was soon apparent that Fate had truly had an appointment with Jim.

Is there such an animal as an authentic Irish drunk? I've known a few drunks of Irish extraction, Americans with a firm Irish ancestry, or possibly Scotch-Irish. Wow…talk about snot-running drunk. And let there be no equivocations: Jim Morrison could put away three times as much booze as anyone else. Three times. I'm not kidding. I'm reasonably convinced the booze killed him in the end. Two nights of snorting China White heroin may have been the final nail in his coffin. *May* have. No one knows for sure, or will ever know.

Seven years later, fresh out of Indiana University, I hopped into a sky-blue Ford van loaded with almost everything I owned, including a Hammond organ, a Fender Rhodes piano, amps—the typical arsenal of a future rock star. I was being pulled across the country by that huge fame magnet known as Los Angeles. Not taking the direct route, the drive was long, taking about a week, and by the time I reached the L.A. suburb of Westwood I had visited friends in Mississippi, Texas and Redding, California.

I rented a motel room—it might have been a Howard Johnsons—locked the van, locked the room and hibernated for twenty-four hours. I definitely had mixed emotions about being back in L.A. There I was, just little 'ol me against this sprawling metropolis. HELP!!!

I eventually ended up in a small Hollywood apartment, way up on North Gower Street. Whenever I was suffering from a bad hangover, I could walk just one block behind and through a gate onto the former Errol Flynn estate. Following the winding lane uphill, I could see the old tennis court and the foundation of the house, surrounded by plenty of trees and overgrown foliage. I could also easily imagine the wild parties that took place there in the Forties and Fifties. Through the pain of my occasional hangovers, I could feel a connection to Flynn's misspent life. There, on that deserted hill, I somehow felt a degree of solace. Being alone for a while, in the midst of millions of people, helped.

I put together a phone list and eventually spoke with quite a number of show business people, most of which had to wonder, *Who the hell is Doug Cameron?* I played piano in a few clubs, and for a while played for five hours a night at the Shakey's Pizza Parlor in Pasadena. I lost that gig because I played too much blues. Evidently family restaurants and the blues do not mix, not even in California. Generally, I struggled.

Every now and then I would call Ray Manzarek or Robby Krieger and have a brief chat. Robby, who was always encouraging, would tell me about how he was hanging around with the band Toto. *Toto Schmoto*, I thought. *They can't touch the Doors.* And I told him so. John Densmore's number had changed by the time I returned to Los Angeles, so I only saw him once or twice at the Cherokee Studios recording facility.

It was at Cherokee that I was provided with a clear picture of how *not* being ready when opportunity strikes can be exasperating. In early June, exactly nine years to the month after I'd first hit the road with the Doors, Ray invited me to a recording session at Cherokee. He, Robby and John were working with producer/engineer John Haeny to assemble an album of Jim's poetry, interwoven with old and new music by, of course, the Doors. When I arrived at the studio, Ray and John Haeny were sitting behind the recording console, and a few seconds after I joined them in the booth—BOOM! A huge crash of thunder blasted from the speakers. Ray recoiled sideways in his chair. I could not believe the shot my ears had just taken. When I recovered I quickly realized that we were listening to the original thunderstorm track used for *L.A. Woman's* "Riders On the Storm." Evidently the same sound effect was being considered for use on the poetry album.

Toward dusk, Robby and John Densmore showed up. The five of us settled in around the console to listen to a playback of the work that had been done thus far when Ray asked me if I had read the works of a particular poet.

"Never heard of him," I said. "Have you ever read *In My Soul I Am Free* by Paul Twitchell?"
"Nope."
"You know—Eckankar and all of that. Eckankar is known as the Ancient Science of Soul Travel. It's a rare religion. Some friends of mine are into it, back home. It's astral projection."
"I've heard of something like that," said Robby. "Buddhist, isn't it?"
"Yes," I said. "It's along those lines."

The philosophical discussion continued when I began quibbling with Densmore about how without Stravinsky's *The Rite of Spring* there would have been no Elvis, and with no Elvis, no Beatles. The Russian composer's piece was so radically unlike anything heard before that, when first performed in Paris in 1913, the audience went wild. I remarked that *Rite* was atonal.

"No, it isn't," John said.
"Oh, you're right," I said. "It was just dissonant."
"That's right."
Man, I thought, *this cat knows his music history.*

Later, after we'd devoured nearly an entire basket of fruit, I joined Robby and John in the studio, which contained only a grand piano. John was noodling idly up and down the keyboard, playing some nondescript stuff.

"Get up," Robby said. "I want to hear this kid play."

John surrendered the piano to me, and I ran through two or three Doors tunes, ending with a short rendition of Willie Dixon's "Back Door Man," complete with vocal. I won't go into how I altered the lyrics, but I suspect Jim would have approved of my substitutions.

"Steamed my jeans, huh?" said Robby.
"I did change it a bit," I said.
"Maybe you should sing Jim's parts on this new record," John kidded.
"Yeah, right," I replied.
"Ya got any original stuff?" John asked.
"Well, yeah." I proceeded to play a Latin thing called "Spangled Gong" that I had written in Germany in 1970. It was not one of my better efforts, and without a full band and various effects, it came off lukewarm.
"Anything else?" Robby asked.
"There's a jazz tune I'm still working on called 'Introducing Sam Smiley.' It goes like this." I tried to play what I had at the time, but the melody line wasn't finished, so I couldn't give a complete performance. The tune, loosely based on a quixotic playwright/professor I'd studied with at Indiana University in 1974-75, was vague, as were its reasons.

Robby and John seemed mildly impressed, but really didn't say much. It didn't take me more than a few seconds to realize that I had BLOWN IT! Man, these cats were two of the Doors, millionaires. So it was that I learned an important lesson: Don't put the cart before the horse. I had wanted to be as famous as the Doors, but I placed too much emphasis on fame. And fame is the cart. The horse is passion, passion for the music in the cart. The cart does not pull the horse. I had it wrong. I didn't believe in my own talent. Now I know. The Doors once had a real reason, a catalyst who was an emotional thunderstorm, a storm named Jim Morrison.

Years later, standing in the crew area of a 767 flying six miles above the Pacific Ocean, two hours out from Maui, I happened to think of a book I'd recently read: *The Jim Morrison Scrapbook*, compiled by the Morrison and Courson families. There's a picture in there of Jim and his family in their Sunday best, standing on the lawn in front of their house, probably in Alexandria, Virginia. Everything appears normal…except for the expression on Jim's face, as if he's expecting a major thunderstorm to erupt at any moment. What fires must have stoked the furnace that was Jim Morrison. Beyond anything else he may have been, he was an incredible study in the history of genius. He was also, as John Densmore once said to me, "the saddest person I ever knew."

I was invited back to Cherokee Studios for the premiere of Jim's posthumous poetry album, *An American Prayer*, shortly before its November 1978 release. It was a real charge to see John, Robby and Ray again. Producer John Haeny was there, as were Frank Lisciandro, Danny

Sugerman (latter day manager of the Doors), Babe Hill (Jim's legendary drinking buddy) and maybe half a dozen others. I sat next to Robby as the first cut, "Awake," faded in: "Is everybody in?" Jim asked. That voice…it was eerie, as if Jim was hiding somewhere in the shadows of the dimly lit studio. I felt the album was a triumph, and couldn't help but wonder what Jim would have thought.

As I was leaving, I showed Ray, Robby and John the photos I had taken during my tenure as a Doors roadie nine years before. When they spotted the former Julia Densmore in one, they all bellowed raucously, especially John. I asked if it would be all right if someone took my picture with them. There was a unanimous "No." Well, the Doors always were known for being somewhat chilly. That had obviously not changed. After that night I never saw the surviving Doors together again.

I can't discuss my time in L.A. circa 1969, then 1978-79, without talking about Ray Manzarek. Ray is basically a decent guy who is quick to pick up on "the rub." By this I mean he is very smart and very talented. And, at times, his ego is very large. I knew him far better than Robby and John. Ray and I spent many hours on long distance calls between Indiana and California, though it wasn't as though he really wanted me to contact him.

One day in 1975, struck by one of my random bright ideas, I called Mercury Records in Los Angeles. Ray was currently under contract to Mercury for the Golden Scarab project, and though I explained who I was, no one at the company would give me his number. Fine. I called Mercury in New York. Boom! They gave me the number after a simple explanation: "Hi, I'm Doug Cameron, and I used to be part of the Doors' road crew. I'm trying to catch up with my friend, Ray Manzarek." Voila!

I called Ray's number one evening and ended up speaking with his mother-in-law, who was babysitting. She was very pleasant, so we chatted for a while. I mentioned that I was also hoping to talk to Robby and John, and she graciously supplied me with their phone numbers. Thank you, Mrs. Fujikawa! And it didn't end there. I also acquired the numbers of both homes owned by Corky and Penny Courson, the parents of Jim's common-law wife, Pam.

Through many years of phone conversations I became privy to a great deal of insider information that most Doors fans still don't know. For instance, Ray and I were talking about the song "Spanish Caravan" when I remarked, "That is such a great tune. I love the guitar work. Why didn't you guys have a long guitar solo in the middle?"

"We tried, man," said Ray. "The solo just wasn't good."
"Wow…"
"Yeah, it was, frankly, quite bad."

Whenever I'd call at an inconvenient moment, Ray would invariably snap, "Now is not a good time, man!" In retrospect, I believe there were a couple of occasions when I'd intruded on an *intimate* moment. I would quickly excuse myself and hang up. Oops! Sorry, Ray…

Sometimes I had a "clever" way of putting my foot in my mouth, such as the time Robby called me in Bloomington, Indiana, where I was almost done working on my Baccalaureate degree.

"Cameron's Clodhoppers," I answered.
"Hello. This is Robby." A tropical bird of some sort screeched in the background.

Yes, it was Robby Krieger calling from his home in Los Angeles, wanting to know what I had wanted when I called him a couple of days earlier. Simply put, I just wanted to bullshit, to keep up with what he was doing. We talked briefly, and then he rang off. From what I understand now, Robby never answers his phone. Anyone wishing to speak to him has to send a FAX stating the number and purpose of the call. He might call back...but probably not.

I rarely talked with John Densmore. His temper seemed more mercurial, quick to anger. But we had a couple of good conversations, and I once told him that I wanted to be a rock star.

"Why would you want all that pressure?" he asked.
"I don't know," I replied. "I guess I didn't look at it from that angle."

Of course we talked about Jim. I have come to feel that John was the most concerned about Jim's well-being, and was also the most troubled by the virtual cornucopia of strange sexual and amoral events that swirled around the Doors on an almost daily basis.

"Jim was the most unhappy person I ever knew," John once said, repeating what he'd already told me on another occasion. "It was like he was carrying around a huge medicine ball on his shoulders all the time."
"I think you're right," I said. "Everyone wonders why."

One of the things I admire about John is his honesty, and his book, *Riders On the Storm*, is among the top three of the many written about the Doors.

I had an indirect involvement with director Oliver Stone's the film *The Doors*. During one of my conversations with Ray, I mentioned that I had picked up a Vox Continental organ. He immediately expressed interest in buying it because nobody in L.A. had one. We agreed on a price, and I received a check from his accountants. I boxed up the organ and a schematic, and shipped it off to Beverly Hills. It's the same one used in *The Doors*. Only a year before it had been stored in my parents' garage in Kokomo, Indiana.

Actually, the story behind my acquisition of the Vox is one of my favorites. I was working in Lafayette, Indiana, where there is a small business newspaper called The Recycler. It has a huge listing of everything one can imagine. While perusing the Piano/Organ section, I found the Vox being advertised by a party in Brazil, Indiana. I called the number. Yes, said a woman, the organ was still for sale, and there was also a Vox amplifier available. The equipment belonged to her son, and it had been stored in her garage for several years. I drove over to her house, we agreed on a price, and I bought the organ and the amp. At home, I discovered that the latter did not work, so I had to use my keyboard amp to test the organ. It worked, but there were many problems with the keys. Anyone who has played a Vox Continental knows how fragile and poorly made they were. Like Farfisa organs, I seem to recall them being manufactured in Italy. Regardless of who made them, they were not built to last. Ray used a Vox Continental on the Doors' first album and, I believe, the second one as well. By the third album, he was using a Gibson Kalamazoo, which I like more. A Gibson has one of the best sounds in all of rock 'n' roll. It's what Ray played in concert from 1968 on, including, of course, the night I first met the band on November 3, 1968.

The Gibson Kalamazoo was instrumental—no pun intended—in getting my name slapped onto millions of Doors albums. I was visiting my daughter, Leslie, on Long Island, and during the week I drove into the city and checked out a Sam Ash store. Sam Ash sells used musical instruments, and inside this particular store, in a long row of various keyboards, was a Gibson Kalamazoo organ. BOOM! BANG! BONG! I bought that keyboard with absolutely no hesitation. And it sounded righteous. I played it for about a year in my band called Roadhouse, back in Bloomington, Indiana. The gigs were few. The next time I spoke with Ray, sometime in 1983, I mentioned the organ, and he asked how much I wanted for it. I quoted a price, and he didn't flinch. Frankly, I sold the damn thing way too cheap. I boxed it myself, tossed in a schematic, and sent it off to Hollywood. Part of the deal was that if Ray ever decided to sell it, I'd be given first opportunity. HA! HA! Oh, sure…

I soon learned through the Doors' grapevine that Ray, Robby and John were compiling a second live album, even though Jim had been dead for twelve years. When I talked to Ray again, I flat out asked if I could be mentioned in the album credits. "Okay," he said, "but send a postcard to remind me." I did. A couple of months later, my girlfriend Brier and I picked up a new copy of *Alive She Cried* by the Doors. I checked the inner sleeve. ZAP! There, among several other names, was mine…Doug Cameron. Hot diggity-damn! Brier and I sat in my car, parked in front of a grocery store in Bloomington, Indiana, and laughed and laughed. WOW! Merry Christmas.

I learned later that Ray had blown a few clams—wrong notes—during the original concert recordings, and had used my Gibson to correct them in the studio. He eventually told me that he had donated the keyboard to an orphanage, which was not all right with me. I'll find another Gibson Kalamazoo someday, but I wanted mine back.

In the past I have stuck up for Ray to the detriment of other friendships. In the Eighties he was scheduled to appear on David Letterman's show, but the show ran too long and Ray was bumped to the following night. Of course, I was watching. With only fifteen minutes left, Letterman brought out a very dim-witted woman phrenologist who claimed the ability to predict a person's future by feeling the bumps on their head. I was pissed. By the time Ray came on, Dave had time for only two or three questions. BAM! The show was over. I called Dorothy and told her what happened. "Oh, no!" she said.

When I talked to Ray later, he told me what he and Letterman had talked about during the commercial break:

"Do you know some guy from Indiana named Doug?" Dave had asked.

"Cameron," said Ray. "Yeah. He was a roadie for us back in the Sixties."

"Plays piano."

"Yep, that's right."

I took it upon myself to write Dave a letter critical of the way Ray had been handled for two nights running. David Letterman is quite sensitive to criticism, so my letter didn't do my relationship with him any good. I'll tell you something about David Letterman; he can't stand being around people. I don't mean to indict him, but he is incredibly private.

As for how relations between Ray and I ended up, the proverbial straw that finally broke the camel's back was a phone call I made to him around Christmas, 1995. There had been a birthday party for John Densmore at John's house, and I had learned that a fight broke out between Ray and John. I took the plunge and pressed the issue with Ray.

"So, Ray, what the hell happened at John's birthday party?"

"Look, man," he said, "you're not my psychiatrist, okay? Can I please just get back to watching my TV?"

Oops! I had run off course. What I suspect is that John was berating Ray for not letting Jim quit the band in 1968 *and* 1969, which was when Jim had been flirting with a nervous breakdown and wanted to quit. That was the same time Ray unashamedly begged Jim to give the band six more months. This is pure speculation on my part. At any rate, Ray changed his number soon after, and we lost touch.

Ray Manzarek has shown my family many kindnesses over the years, and even though I really don't have a relationship with him anymore, I still must thank him. Thanks, Ray…

The relationship between John and the Manzareks has been rocky at times. Dorothy and Ray have a certain opinion about John's anger issues, and feel that John hates them. I won't go into specifics.

As far as Robby and John are concerned, they were friends from the early days. John brought Robby into the band, and they always roomed together on tour, but I wonder how things are between them now. John sued Ray and Robby and the rest of a new band Ray and Robby had decided to call the Doors. Jim's parents also sued over the same issue. The contention of the plaintiffs was that if Ray, Robby and John are not performing together onstage, no other combination of musicians can be called the Doors. John and the Morrisons won the case. Ray and Robby's band is now called Riders On the Storm.

Robby Krieger was the last member of the Doors I met with before I bade farewell to L.A. As he aged, Robby became known as The Geezer, or The Ghost, and I found him to be camera shy due to his geezerness. Once, when I reminded him that he had not yet given me a promised copy of his *Robby Krieger & Friends* album on the Blue Note label, he invited me up to his house. He lived in one of the canyons, and after I was allowed to drive through the security gate, he met me at the back door. How fitting…Back Door Man. We passed through the kitchen, which contained a large tank of tropical fish, and went into Robby's study at the front of the house. The far wall was completely taken up by bookshelves. In the right hand corner was an area filled with record albums, including a copy of *Robby Krieger & Friends*. He pulled the record out of the cover and noticed there was no sleeve. He shoved the unprotected slab of vinyl back in, and said, "Oh, well. Here ya go."

"Holy Hanukkah, Robby. Thank you so much!"

"Sure."

I noticed a spinet piano against the front wall of the room. "Nice piano. Mind if I try it?"

"Go ahead," said Mr. Spanish Caravan.

I played a few progressions from a couple of Doors tunes.

"Not bad for a white guy," Robby said.

"Actually, I'm black, Robby. See my eyes? They're brown. I ain't no blue-eyed soul brother. My skin? Well, junior high school swim teams…the chlorine. My skin just got lighter and lighter."

"Well, there ya go, Douglas."

"Right."

I adroitly realized I was being asked to leave. I'd barely arrived. We walked back through the kitchen, and when we reached the back door I asked Robby if we could take a picture together.

"No, man," he said. "I don't do close-ups anymore."

"All right, man. Well, thank you very much."

We shook hands, and within a few seconds I was in my van, driving south through the canyon. Despite the brevity of our meeting, and the less than mint condition of the record, I thought, *Man, Robby is really one nice cat.* I still have the album. After I heard it, I gave him a call and told him he had buried himself too far down in the mix.

"I know it," he said. "Everybody's told me that."

"I really liked that one about Marilyn Monroe. It's my favorite. You were on to something there."

"Well, Blue Note went belly-up right after the album was released, so there was no promotion. It crashed."

"Is there any way to remix it and re-release it on a different label?"

"Doubt it," said the composer of "Light My Fire."

"Anyway, I hope you mix your guitar tracks and your vocals stronger on your next album. Bring out that barking seal sound you got on 'Not To Touch the Earth,' you know?"

"Barking seal…yeah."

So long, Robby. John…Ray…Los Angeles…

***

– 14 –

THE COURSONS

Thanks to Dorothy Fujikawa-Manzarek's mother, I was able to speak with the parents of the late Pamela Courson on two occasions, both in 1981. Corky and Penny Courson proved to be affable and right upfront. I told them I was considering writing a book about my experiences with the Doors and asked if they would mind answering a few questions. At first they seemed suspicious. Penny wanted to know if I was working on behalf of Ray Manzarek. His album *The Golden Scarab* had just been released, and in the course of discussing the cover, Penny remarked, "That goddamn Pollack had to paint his face gold to sell any records." I was genuinely surprised. There was some major enmity there.

"No, no, no," I said. "I'm not working for Ray. We're acquainted, but not close friends." I asked if it would be all right to quote them. "That would be fine," Corky replied.

During a conversation that lasted about an hour, I listened carefully as they told me how, at first, they were quite leery of Jim. They talked about their daughter's personal struggles in high school during the early to mid-Sixties.

"Jim was no paragon of virtue," Penny said.
"As we began to know Jim better, Pamela brought some of his poetry around," said Corky. "We had already started to take him seriously, as an artist. He was always so quiet."
"He told Pam they were afraid their little goldfish was going to swim away," Penny said, referring to the other Doors.

Eventually we got around to the subject of Jim's death. "Jim came back to the apartment around midnight, complaining of chest pains," said Corky. "Pam drew him a hot bath, and went back to bed. Around two a.m. she called to him but got no response. So she got out of bed and found him dead in the tub, with a grin on his face."

"What was the address of the apartment?" I asked.
"Nineteen rue Beautrellis," Corky replied. (Actually it was seventeen rue Beautrellis.)
"There seems to be such a mystery about Jim's death," I said. "From what I understand, there are two types of heart attacks: coronary thrombosis and myocardial infarction. If the coronary thrombosis is euphoric, as I've heard, that would explain the grin."

"It wasn't easy for Pamela," said Penny. "When she finally came home the next week, she must have sat on the couch for forty-eight hours talking non-stop about what happened in Paris."

"Did you know Jim had asthma?" I asked.

"Yes," said Corky. "We did know that."

"Vince told me that only recently," I added. "You know who Vince is, don't you?"

"Yes," said Penny.

"So," I continued, "Jim's coughing up blood, experiencing chest pain, smoking cigarettes, still drinking heavily, suffering from asthma, and now he is in a hot bathtub. His heart couldn't take anymore."

"It was a fatal mix," Corky agreed.

"I understand that Pamela died in 1974," I said. "Approximately two and a half years after Jim. I'm very sorry for your loss."

"Thank you, Doug," said Penny.

"Yes," Corky said, "thank you."

"I don't think she ever got over Jim," said Penny.

"I agree with you," I replied.

"Did you know Pamela?" asked Corky.

"No, sir. I did meet her once, but it was very brief. We barely spoke."

When I asked the Coursons what it had been like when they met Jim's parents, Penny's response was to the point: "They have lost a son, and we have lost a daughter."

"But doesn't the distance between Jim and his parents seem strange?" I asked. "I mean, it's just not natural."

"Let me tell you," said Corky. "Jim was very big on the young lion leaving the pride. It was very important to him. He talked about it often."

"I know a lot about the Doors," I said. "I consider myself something of a Doorsologist."

"Well, you don't know it all, buddy," said Penny. "Did you ever hear about the car ride in New York? No? Jim tried to strangle Ray! John and Robby had to restrain Jim, or he would have killed Ray."

"Holy shit!" I said.

"It's the truth," said Corky.

"Damn sure was a power struggle between them," I said.

As the conversation continued, I couldn't believe my good fortune. I was learning things I thought only the inner circle—way inside the fire—knew. I tried to return to the subject of Jim's parents, asking the Coursons how the Morrisons were doing.

"We met with them shortly after Pamela's passing," said Penny. "We, at that time, took steps to share Jim and Pam's estate with the Morrisons, fifty-fifty."

The more I spoke with the Coursons, the more I liked them. They were genuine, and occasionally raucous. Especially Penny. But, to be sure, there was a sorrow to them that I felt almost immediately.

"Were there any of Jim's books left?" I asked.

"Yes, hundreds," said Corky. "But one of the most surprising things that we returned to the Morrisons was a sword that belonged to his father. Jim had kept it."

"Wow! Was it a saber, or a sword?"

"It was a naval officer's dress sword. It looked old to me."

Man, I thought. *A sword...talk about some heavy symbolism...*

My second interview with the Coursons was not long, and Penny went way above and beyond in making sure that they were not going to approve anything of an artistic nature regarding the Doors. I later learned that by 1995 the Coursons' attorneys had been presented with a number of proposed Doors projects subject to the Coursons' approval. One by one, Corky and Penny turned all of them down. Fortunately, they had not said no to me in 1981.

Thank you, Mr. and Mrs. Columbus Courson.

* * *

– 15 –

VINCE TREANOR REVISITED

Vincent Treanor III was brilliant when it came to building pipe organs, building amplifiers—such as the Monolith stage system first used by the Doors at Chicago's Auditorium Theatre on June 14, 1969—or setting up assembly lines for amplifier production, as he did for Acoustic Amplifier Company. He is also very manipulative and, basically, by now, an old queen. The tricks he pulled trying to impress me, using my fascination with the Doors as a catalyst, are nearly unbelievable.

In the very first letter I received from Vince in November 1968, he asked: "How was it that Jim Morrison told me to hire you?" This was a very large load of manure. In the last letter, which I received in 1974, he asked—and I paraphrase—"Where were you? Jim waited to put a new band together and wanted you to play the keyboards." The Doors were aware of my musical abilities, but I feel that this bit from the '74 letter was also pure fantasy. Jim was so burned out by 1971. To think that he wanted to put another band together is ludicrous. He had created this rock star image that became his albatross. Now he could get that dead bird from around his neck.

Over a period of seven years I received seven letters from Vince, now of South Korea. Unfortunately, I lost the first and last ones. It's too bad because letter number seven really was incredible. Four of the five letters have been included in this book, and they do give some interesting history of the Doors, especially around the time of the infamous March 1, 1969 concert at the Dinner Key Auditorium.

Beginning in 1974 and every few years after, I would get in touch with Vince. I must say that he gave me quite a bit of inside information about the Doors that I have shared with various people. The last time we talked he told me he still owned much of the equipment used by the band—all of the microphones, two transformers for the Monolith amplifiers, and the gold Electro Voice 676 microphone visible on some color posters of the Jim, circa 1967. Vince said he was asking $50,000 for everything, and I later found it interesting that neither Ray nor Oliver Stone bought it for the film. They both knew it was available. When I asked Ray about it, he said, "Who could verify that it was the genuine article? Fifty-thousand? He's dreaming."

In the Seventies and Eighties, Vince became involved with building sailboats at Marina del Ray. Toward the end of that time, he sold his autographed copy of *The New Lords and Creatures*,

Jim's first book of poetry, for $10,000. He then moved to Thailand, returning to the United States several years later, with a newly adopted Chinese son.

While in L.A. in July of 2008, my wife, Fran, and I did an exhaustive amount of detective work and finally located Vince in South Korea. After he realized who I was, he kindly consented to an "interview" of sorts, answering questions—via a series of letters—that had been on my mind for almost forty years, including the substance of what he and Jim had discussed in the workshop so long ago. When I informed him that I was working on a book about my time with the Doors, he recalled that period as "a bad summer all around, with the results of the Miami debacle."

The last time Vince and I spoke, he said, "You never paid the price." By this, of course, he meant that I hadn't dropped the shower room soap in his vicinity. I told him I wouldn't have paid that price in fifty-five quintillion years. Even though he was, in my experience, devious, Vince's eventual firing by Bill Siddons was cold. Vince didn't deserve to be treated that way. But, with Jim dead, the Doors' star was no longer ascending. Vince was expendable.

What follows are Vince's recollections. And, to be fair, whatever else occurred between us forty years ago, I very much appreciate his help.

* * *

SINCE 1969

I moved from Durand Drive to Hollywood proper, and then to Venice. After that I was in Taiwan for two years, China for four, and now Korea since 2000. I pretty much divorced myself from the music industry after Bill Siddons screwed me.

THE WORKSHOP

I guess 8512 has been radically modified since 1972. That is when the Doors finally abandoned the place. It has been a restaurant, and I think the last report was another refit as another restaurant, but a lot has been changed within the building and surrounding area. I have not seen it for at least fourteen years. I have been in Korea for the last eight years. Not certain of the future. The past is just memories.

HIS MEMOIRS

I have written down some of the events of my time with the group. I thought I might get it published. The guy who was going to help abandoned the effort, so I have not pursued it. The book languishes in the hard drive of my computer. I don't know what to do about it. There are far too many books out, in any case. Ray and John have written. Frank Lisciandro, Paul Ferrara, and I'm not sure who else. Robby and Ray are playing together. John is not speaking to either of them—the result of a dispute over the use of the name of the group. Anyway, I really have no idea what to do with the book. Some say it is too long, though only half done. I wonder what to put in and what not. It is difficult to work all day long and then try to sit down and get one's head into divulging ancient history. There are, of course, key moments of agony and ecstasy, but even those are fading into the past. What is the difference to anyone, anyway? So many people have written so much about a group they did not really know and a person no one really understood. I don't know what to do about the book. It is not highest on my things to do list.

GROUP CONFLICTS

The comments in Ray's book about Jim wanting John out of the group are what caused the split between John and Ray. This has been further exacerbated by the lawsuit between Ray and Robby against John and the Coursons. All in all, it is a sad affair, and most hurtful that three guys who were so much together way back have come to such a pass.

John, after the debacle at Isle of Wight, was the first of the group to speak out about not wanting to play with Jim in public again. This was further confirmed after the New Orleans performance. At that point, the three boys were in agreement that they would not again play with Jim. He was to be part of the writing and recording team, but nothing onstage, where they could have a situation.

Remember that the Isle of Wight was the lead performance of a series throughout Europe. It was canceled as a result of the Florida trial. Once again, their financial and artistic wellbeing was negatively influenced by Jim's bad behavior. The abysmal performance, on top of the strain of the trial and then the cancellation of the tour, did not sit well. It did plant the seeds of discontent that boiled over when they returned to L.A. Jim was then told that public performances were out. He promised to amend his ways, and asked Bill to book two or three shows—Dallas and New Orleans. Of course, Dallas was mediocre, and New Orleans was a drunken disaster.

Anyway, it was not really Jim who wanted John out. Rather, it was John and Robby who wanted Jim out of the public eye. But they did not want to break up the group. They were only to be a recording group. It was the summer of '71 when *Other Voices* came into being, almost before Jim set foot on the plane to Paris. That venture came to a disastrous end about eighteen months later, as a result of the unpopularity of the music Ray insisted on playing.

I always hoped the guys would get together after the Stone movie. They were together at that time, all of them. Then Ray had to publish his book, which was possibly informative regarding background and experiences, but it somewhat glossed over the bad points, causes and results.

OLIVER STONE'S *THE DOORS*

The Stone movie was a disaster, a travesty. Ray refused to participate in the shambles that Stone was making of the Doors' story. He and Stone disagreed on many points, and Ray went public. Stone had no choice but to get into a public debate in the media or separate himself from Ray. John, Robby and I went along with it in the hope that something could be done to influence Stone into a more realistic position. He was after fantasy, not reality. As a result, the movie suffered. The chance to tell the real story of Miami was not told. Nor were the New Haven or Las Vegas stories. I worked as an advisor on the film, and though every effort was made to guide Stone along the more accurate and interesting version, he wanted to follow the fantasy life he created for Jim. Basically an Oliver Stone fantasy based on the Sugerman fantasy.

DANNY SUGERMAN

What could that kid have known? He was only sixteen when Jim died. He wrote *No One Here Gets Out Alive* and became the Doors' manager, eventually embezzling a lot of money to satisfy a cocaine habit. He died a few years ago. He was a groupie who took advantage of a situation and wormed his way into the organization. He had it good until he took advantage of it.

THE EQUIPMENT

The equipment that I had—all the mics, six acoustic amps and the AC electrical equipment—was stolen in 2003. Some of it turned up on various auction sites, and the rest disappeared. In addition, I lost my camera, Snap On tools and a lot of other equipment. The acoustic system and the amps I built for the group were all sold. There is no history of what happened after that. The prop people for the movie did what they could to locate the original equipment, to no avail. Everything, except the standard Acoustic amps, was a reproduction. However, the mic stands, cords, mixer and such that were seen in the film were authentic and original.

THE PRIVATE WORKSHOP CONVERSATION WITH JIM
(ABOUT MIAMI)

We discussed the warrant, the reason for it (political) and the possible outcome. He was surprised to learn that I had been behind him holding his pants up, at the behest of Ray. He was so drunk that he did not really remember all the events of that night. The probability of any more warrants was really not a big factor since he had done about everything he could under the circumstances—actually, Max Fink took care of the case and all the legal wrangling that went on. Jim was less worried about more warrants than the outcome of the initial arrest on various points of drunk and public lewd behavior. He was also very interested in what transpired with the promoter and the equipment, why we did not cancel. Of course, all the guys were angry with Bill for getting into the deal with the guy, who had a bad reputation for payment and was a known cheat.

BILL SIDDONS

Bill was the Doors' "yes" man. His contract gave him the power of attorney to act for the group in business matters. However, he was not given the independence of decision or action that other managers had. He was held in check in that he had to present any and all matters before the group, and was bound by their collective or majority decision. He had to have their permission to do anything. He used his position to promote other shows—and some of the Doors'—and even became manager of another group. Unconfirmed rumor has it that they went nowhere, but the fault may not have been with Bill. As you know, with so many young musicians, luck is everything. Talent is incidental to good promotion, good looks, fantastic physiques. Even a recent fad—tattoos—count more than the ability to sing, play an instrument, or present a good performance.

I have felt strongly that there was a constant strain between Bill and Jim. Jim was the only member of the group who pushed me to take the manager's job, in April 1968. Bill was very bitter about that, and eventually took revenge on me in 1972. I have long felt that the disrespect that Bill showed towards Jim, as well as his general attitude and comments, had much to do with Jim's decline and growing indifference toward the group. They never got along. I saw and heard Bill do and say things that would have gotten him fired had be been talking to me. Bill was lucky it would have taken a full agreement of all four guys to fire him. It is true that Bill was essentially a puppet. He did make many propositions and offer many suggestions that led the group into bad or weak positions. Miami is the classic example, and refusing the request of Bill Graham to help out in January 1969.

JIM

Jim was the product of a military background. He was like his brother and sister, under his father's control. He moved about a lot as his father was posted to various military bases. He made no real or lasting relations, male or female, during his time in school or on the bases, mainly because of the short time he was there. Whatever bond was formed was broken as he moved on. There is one story about his going out on the aircraft carrier task force on a training mission. Here was this giant ship and all the auxiliary vessels in the task force. At the simple command from his father, all these ships and all the men on them acted on that command. Here is this enormous force of military ships, thousands of men, and unthinkable numbers of terrible and most powerful weapons. And this one man, his father, had control over it all. One simple man. He had the power and authority to wipe out whole cities, millions of people influenced for untold decades. Just this one man. I firmly believe that this bent Jim. He could not grasp how this could come to be. It may have been part of the rebellion that Jim perpetrated. He could "fight the system."

It is known that even in school he was a loner. He did not mix well, and was always doing things to bring attention to himself. This showed in his behavior in later life as well. People are giving him credit for pushing the boundaries of society. It was not necessarily a real test of human endurance or exploration. His "push" was in the form of offending the public or behaving in a manner that would attract attention.

He was charismatic. He started riots. He did nothing that anyone with a thinking mind and a microphone cannot do. Using that same mic, I stopped a few riots, or prevented a few from getting worse. The point is that Jim was saying things people wanted to hear but were afraid to attempt. Even Jim did not follow his own advice, except when it was convenient. He spoke of liberation, freedom, experimentation and open minded concepts. In most of these he failed to follow through. In some, he did to useless excess. Jim used the stage to be wanted, and people paid attention to him. He had people who made him famous, important. These things he never had before he went public. He was the son of a military man, living a military life through his father. His mother coddled him, was oppressive and controlling. He finally realized the crowd wanted to see his antics—but not the bullshit. He came to the awareness that they did not care about him as a person, but as a sex symbol, someone who advocated a sort of revolution and was constantly in trouble for bungling the propaganda he spread. He was against the Establishment, and for people growing up facing what seemed like an unending stream of war, death and destruction, Morrison was making some sense. The Establishment had gotten them into this mess. Maybe Morrison didn't have the proper answers, but he had an alternative, and that was better than going to Vietnam.

It is my opinion that Jim never intended to die from the use of drugs or anything else. He was not that emotionally strong. The use of heroin was just another step in his anti-social behavior, and another one of the outward manifestations of rebellion. However, you cannot write or create while under the influence of such a narcotic. Jim was no different. For those to claim that such drugs enhanced the creative experience is foolish. They do not know what they are talking about. In any case, Jim was trying to prove that he also had power. He loved the stage and the ability to talk to the crowd. He enjoyed the power that the mic gave him, and the adoration of the crowds when he poured forth his profundities. Jim, as an individual, was nothing. Just the troubled son of a very important and powerful military officer. True, he liked reading, but look at the material he liked to read. It gave him the basis for his unusual visions of life. One can ask if all the ideals he espoused were really his or an amalgamation of the authors he read. Until the formation of the Doors, he was just another person, unnoticed among thousands in UCLA film school. It was the Doors that gave him an outlet. Fame and money brought individual attention by the media both for his "philosophies" as well as his erratic behavior, both on and offstage. Unfortunately for Jim, his money attracted others who were equally lost and seeking some form of recognition or fame. As long as he had money, they hung around him, enjoying his largess, and goaded him along. When the money ran out, they went to a different pile of garbage like the gadflies they were. Note that even Paul Ferrara, who sued Jim and the Doors, became a real "pal" after Jim died. There is much talk of Ferrara and his participation in the making of the movie, but little indication of the rancor and bitter feelings raised by Ferrara when he demanded more money from Jim—and consequently, the Doors—for his work on *Hwy*. Today, Ferrara talks about Jim as though nothing ever happened. He is also exploiting his position for financial gain.

Basically, I suppose that a short analysis would demonstrate that Jim was suppressed by the discipline he grew up with, overwhelmed by the stature of his father, and was bent on attracting as much attention to himself as he could. You could ask why Jim went to Paris, made all the noise about leaving the Doors and getting into theater and such. His voice was going, his creative will had just about dried up. Notice the great difference in the tone and theme of his music—not Robby's—after the third album on into *L.A. Woman*, from really lyrical, musically exciting arrangements into some sort of monotonous music. He succumbed to the influence of Ray to change to the Chicago blues style. The audiences did not like this style. It was the change in the group's composition and musical format that brought about the demise of "other voices." Jim could sense that things were not going well. He also, likely, remembered that the group did not need him—clearly demonstrated by the performance without him in Amsterdam. Certainly that was not a comforting situation.

Remember that after the Isle of Wight performance, Jim told the group that he could straighten out and get back to business. He was well aware of their dissatisfaction with his behavior and lack of performance onstage. No one has attributed this talk of breaking away from the singing into the theater as a defensive measure to cover the growing rift between himself and the other guys. This is further reinforced by his call to John, maybe a test situation, telling John that he was feeling better and was ready to get back to performing and recording again.

Jim craved the attention and he had gotten used to the money, the fame, and the power of his presence onstage. That never goes away once you have tasted it. Rock stars do not "retire." They always hang around the community, often being reborn through a reunion of the group, or a continuing—though not often successful—performing or recording career. Jim was just a guy who was frustrated, lonely, insecure, a confirmed alcoholic, drug abuser, and addicted to the material things that money could buy. Jim was in conflict with his fear of failure and desire for the money that his "career" brought him.

Without Ray, John and Robby, Jim would have remained a nobody. Certainly his films were of little note, and he was more of a joke in UCLA than anyone to be taken seriously. Ray, John and Robby could have had a very successful performing band with anyone who wrote the material that Jim did, and was as dramatic as Jim was onstage. Jim was just the right guy at the right time with the right music. Remember, however, that the greatest hit the Doors had was written by Robby—not Jim—and was arranged by Ray.

I hope this gives some insight into the complexity that was Jim. Many people have the same background that Jim did. They do not become rebels, alcoholics, and drug abusers. They go through school, maybe not, and become part of a functional society. Jim just decided to be a rebel as a path to recognition. In the end, it was his death that made him more famous, and his memorial is not his writing or "poetry." Rather, the infamy of Miami and all the controversy that surrounded that incident.

THE DEATH OF JIM MORRISON

No matter how Jim died, it was an accident. He did die under very strange circumstances, exacerbated by the inactivity and inefficiency of the Paris police. Lies and disinformation were propagated by those involved. There are so many theories and much speculation. It is difficult to put it all together. It is a fact that Jim was using cocaine before he left for Paris. That was due to the influence of Paul Rothchild. And it is a fact that Pam was an addict and had a regular supplier in the inner circle of acquaintances. It is a fact that her suppliers left Paris in great haste the morning Jim was found dead. It is a fact that no autopsy was performed. The body was packed in ice in the tub where it was found, and was not removed for two or three, or possibly four days after he died, while the Paris police "investigated."

There were lies, cover-up, and all sorts of misleading information passing through every medium and all the people who knew anything. Most of them, of course, wanted to distance themselves from Jim and Pam because of the drug involvement. They would be found to be involved in drugs as users, providers or having knowledge that could implicate others. Basically it was like dropping a ball of mercury—when it hits, the little beads fly everywhere.

There is a timeline, and supposedly it involved Jim going to a bar or place where known dealers were to be found, and known users came to get their supply. Jim was not adverse, as we know from Amsterdam, to using drugs immediately rather than waiting for a more appropriate time or place. Continuing along that line, it is logical to follow one claim that Jim obtained some heroin, ingested it and died, OR BECAME COMATOSE in the toilet of the bar. He was missed by those he was consorting with, and they found him—possibly dead, possibly not—in the stall, and took him home and put him in the tub.

In the whiles, Pam, already having participated in the activity, had remained at the apartment when Jim went out. When she woke up, she found him dead in the tub and started calling friends. From there on, the story is not clear, but certainly a lot less muddy. Was Jim on heroin? It is possible, and probable, given his penchant for trying anything at least once. Did he do it more than once? Quite likely. He went from drink to grass, to drink to acid, to drink to cocaine, to drink to… This is the usual path to Hell, and I have no doubt that he found no excuse not to follow the trend.

PAMELA COURSON

Pam was a completely dysfunctional person. Evidently her parents pampered her, and she never really had to worry about anything. She was used to being taken care of and getting what she wanted. She latched onto Jim and, for some reason many have speculated on but few can understand, Jim was attracted to her. The relationship was something akin to Hitler and Eva Braun. Pam sucked thousands of dollars from Jim for her boutique, in which she sold little and gave away much. And which was really a place for her friends to use drugs and have lengthy and useless social gatherings.

The relationship between her and Jim was never tranquil, becoming more acrimonious and outspoken as time went on. It was a drunk, excused by a riotous fight with Pam, that preceded the Miami incident. Paris was no Sea of Tranquility, either, from first hand reports.

It is likely that, had Jim ever married her, it would have been another Hollywood style incident of public scandal, divorce and a string of successive conquests. Jim had no lack of female followers. It is unlikely that he would ever have made permanent relationships as a result of his youth and the life led as a military brat. He simply had no experience in forming friendships on more than a temporary basis. Likely he was afraid of forming any lasting bond as a result of his youth. Pam found, in Jim, someone who was also dysfunctional, disturbed. Dark. That was likely her attraction to him. She had few friends who had any roots at all, none with a job or a steady income, and certainly none who were famous. Jim paid dearly in cash for her companionship and aggravation. I think, as time went on, this love/hate relationship grew. He was becoming more unhappy with the publicity of his life—which he brought on. She became more cloying, demanding and disruptive. She also did not like the various abuses she suffered, and the frequent transgressions Jim had with other people. Jealous would be the best description. It was a tumultuous relationship. Both were unhappy people from widely different backgrounds and education. Neither really knew what they wanted from life, or how to get it, even if they understood. They possibly needed each other, but why? They hated the relationship and the useless, futile existence they had together. For Pam, Jim was a trophy. For Jim, Pam was willing sex—sometimes.

LEON BARNARD, DOORS PUBLICIST

Leon was also using heroin in 1969 and on. He has written a book about the group. He had a lot of paintings and such that he was trying to sell. I think he is still trying to be successful as an artist. I don't know where he gets his money from. I met him again on the movie set. Leon was a funny guy, seemingly always happy, but inside—not so much. I have no idea where he is now. Vanished into the realm of obscurity.

PIPE ORGANS

I've always liked classical music. I became interested in learning to play in 1949 or '50. I could not find places to practice. A bankrupt organ company was sold, and for forty dollars I acquired the remnants. For the most part it was a collection of junk, the good stuff being auctioned off for a lot more. In any case, one thing led to another. When I went to Boston University, I met a fellow involved in maintenance. That proved more interesting than liberal arts, and that was what really got things started. The break came in 1967, when I went with the

Doors. It resumed thirty-three years later, when I paid a casual visit to Korea. I just had the thought. I lived in Andover for thirty-three years before I made any really major move. Thirty-three years later, another major move. What's next?

* * *

Swinging 'Doors' Open

By Doug Cameron

It was a cold dry afternoon in November when The Doors came to Chicago. I had been setting up the Acoustic amplifiers, drums, and bass piano with Vincent Treanor III, the road manager of The Doors. We finished right after the first part of the concert finished. The first band was the Holocost. This band, composed of four shaggy-haired musicians, played five long numbers then we all started taking down the Holocost's equipment.

We had just dissembled the Holocost's equipment, and I was standing on the stage looking back at the doorway to the dressing rooms, when I saw John Densmore looking through the doorway. Then I saw Robby Krieger and Ray Manzarek with John. Jim Morrison wasn't there.

Afterwards, following my curiosity, I walked back into the garage of the Coliseum. I saw four beautiful girls standing around a tall long-haired figure. He was wearing black boots, a light blue shirt, and white levis. His hair looked dirty, as if it hadn't been washed in a month. This was Jim Morrison, the lead singer of The Doors.

As I walked toward him, a small fat man walked up to Morrison, carrying a portrait. A girl was following him. The man attracted Jim's attention, and asked him how he liked the portrait that she had painted of him. Jim said, "I like it, it's one of the best I've seen."

After the girl and the fat man had left, I introduced myself to Jim. He was very friendly and I found that the rumors I had heard about him being a drunken bum and a pill-popper were quite untrue.

Thanks to Vincent Treanor III, the road manager of The Doors who I had contacted earlier about helping set up The Doors Acoustic amplifiers, I was also able to meet Ray Manzarek, the organist of The Doors. He was very cordial and interesting to talk to. Being an amateur musician myself, I questioned Ray about playing the organ. He told me to stick with it and practice a lot.

The Doors two body guards kept a close watch on me, and the girls that were with Morrison were also under surveilence. These two men were quite rough and I wouldn't hesitate to say that they performed their tasks quite well.

A man of medium height with long hair, psychedelic pants, and a white T-shirt came out of the mobile home unit that was provided for The Doors to get ready for their concert. This was Robby Krieger, the guitarist for the group, and he had his guitar in his hands. I asked him to play something for me, so he played the chords to Light My Fire and a few notes of the guitar solo in When The Music's Over.

Barney Pip, a disc jockey for radio station WCFL, announced the beginning of The Doors concert. Ray and Robby walked up to the stairway of the stage. They were both concealed by a large curtain. Jim and John were nowhere to be found. When I questioned Robby, he said that they were both preoccupied. Finally,

after the crowd had waited for practically two hours. John Densmore came out followed by Jim Morrison, who was holding a can of beer.

The concert started with The Doors' rendition of "Back Door Man". Some of the numbers in the concert included, "When The Music's Over", "Love Me Two Times", "Celebration Of The Lizard", and "Light My Fire". After the concert, The Doors walked off stage and ran into a huge black cadillac to drive to O'Hare International Airport. After I talked to Vince, he told me that they were going back to Los Angeles for a rest. They had just played in Columbus, Ohio the night before.

Steve Connell and I helped take down everything with Vince, load it into the U-haul van, and load a bunch of books printed in Chicago for The Doors. We said good-bye to Vince and began our long walk through south Chicago to the bus-terminal.

As I looked out the window of the bus thinking about the day's events, I knew that this had been the most exciting adventure of my life.

Although this was my first published journalistic piece, I do not take credit for the headline. Someone else wrote that. I never knew who. Also, the article is misleading about the wait for John and Jim's rest stop before the performance. The wait was not a couple of hours. It was just ten minutes.

This article falls under public domain, so no permission was needed

Bloomington man finally gets

By MIKE LEONARD
Sunday Herald-Times

Now it's easy for Doug Cameron to own up to a dreamy goal he envisioned the first time he heard the haunting power of The Doors in 1967.

"I LIKE TO THINK of this as the epilogue to a dream," he said recently. "After 16 years, I finally made it onto a Doors album."

Cameron, a Bloomington insurance agent, only served as assistant road manager for The Doors during a brief span in 1969. With the death of band leader Jim Morrison in 1971 and the demise of the group shortly thereafter, it seemed improbable the fanciful dream of a 17-year-old musician would ever be realized.

Despite Morrison's death, however, interest in the man and his music has remained. After the discovery of audio tape made for a Danish television appearance in 1968, an intensive search completed in late 1982 produced enough quality tracks for a potential new album of live, previously unreleased Doors music.

That's where Cameron would come in.

After Cameron's stint with The Doors in 1969, he went on to military service, college at Indiana University and a career in insurance. He has worked off and on as a musician in local bands, including one named Roadhouse, but a year ago, he decided, as he put it, to "hang up my guns."

SINCE LEAVING The Doors, Cameron said he has maintained loose contact with band members Robbie Krieger, John Densmore and Ray Manzarek — especially Manzarek.

"I had an old, rare keyboard — a Gibson Kalamazoo — which they stopped making in 1968," he explained. "Ray had a couple of them, which he used with The Doors. About a year ago, I was talking with Ray on the phone and I asked him if he would be interested in buying the keyboard. He was, so I boxed it up in January or February and shipped it out to him (in California).

"I didn't know it at the time," Cameron said, "but he wound up using it for a couple of overdubs on the live album. I think he used it on 'Gloria,' and 'Love Me Two Times.' The album, *Alive She Cried*, was released in August 1983 and has been received with near-universal acclaim from the rock press."

CAMERON NATURALLY is pleased. "I feel like I do have a little bitty sliver of rock and roll history to call my

name on Doors album

own," he said.

A Rockford, Ill., native, Cameron's association with The Doors began when he and some friends arrived early for a Doors concert at the Chicago Stadium on Nov. 3, 1968. They were lucky enough to get recruited to help set up spotlights, which allowed them backstage. Cameron, then 17, struck up a friendship with The Doors' road manager, Vince Traynor. Several months later, Cameron completed high school and joined the band as assistant road manager.

He only worked for the band for a couple of months — citing a sticky personal situation as the reason for leaving the group. It was enough time, however, to become acquainted with the band members, including the enigmatic leader, Jim Morrison.

"It was *heavy*," Cameron said. "I don't mean to be blasphemous but hanging around Jim Morrison was probably similar in a way to hanging around Buddha or Jesus Christ, or someone like that. I don't mean to place them in the same category," he said. "Really, it was probably similar to hanging out with Dionysus.

"BUT IT WAS A VERY, very incredible charisma he had. He'd walk into a room and the whole room would fall silent."

Cameron describes Morrison's personality as "mercurial."

"He could be the warmest, nicest person you'd ever want to meet," he said. "But then sometimes — when he was drinking — he'd treat everyone around him badly. 'Just get the hell out of here — who needs you' kind of stuff."

One incident Cameron remembers

(Page 8, col. 1, this sec.)

CAMERON

Jack Morrison of The Doors is shown at left. At right is the whole group, consisting of, front row, Ray Manzarek, left, and Jim Morrison, and, rear, John Densmore, left, and Robbie Krieger.

After 16 years, Cameron gets name on Doors album

(Continued from page C-1) fondly occurred in Mexico City, where he said The Doors were playing at a large nightclub owned by Javier Castro — Fidel's brother. "Jim and I got drunk together and wound up doing racing starts in the pool at the villa where we were staying. We found out that each of us swam the same events in high school: the 50-yard freestyle and the 100-yard freestyle.

"We just kept diving in, all stretched out,

smacking the water, laughing the whole time," he said.

"SADLY ENOUGH, though, the guy was an unbelievable alcoholic. I don't know how he lived as long as he did," Cameron said.

Morrison died in Paris on July 3, 1971, from what official sources term a heart attack. Although some have alleged Morrison's body was never seen and theorize that he may still be

alive, Cameron says, "there's no way."

He does say that those who paint the Morrison image with a Satanic hue may not be wrong.

"He supposedly was married once to a woman in New York, a witch. It was a satanic ceremony, and the story is that they drank blood, the whole bit.

"I feel he was evil," Cameron said. "He was all things. He was everything he could be and you can paint him any color you want."

I enjoyed meeting Robert Zaltsberg at the Bloomington Herald Times of Bloomington, Indiana, who gave me permission to use the Mike Leonard article that appears here. Thanks Bob!

Strange Days, again

orrison in *The Doors*.   File photo

shallow trip
hip history

Judith Cebula

Movies in Review

Photo by Darcy Chang/Journal and Courier

Doug Cameron's teen-age dreams came true in 1969 when he became a roadie for The Doors.

Roadie can't close The Doors

By JUDITH CEBULA
Journal and Courier

Doug Cameron sips his beer. The stereo in the bar begins to blare "Light My Fire," a signature song from The Doors and a hallmark in Cameron's life.

"See! I'm haunted," he says. Cameron's ghosts are The Doors.

He was 17 years old in 1969, and for three weeks he toured with the band as a roadie — plugging in amplifiers and fetching fried chicken for singer Jim Morrison.

They are bittersweet memories.

Cameron had dreamed of becoming a musician and welcomed the brush with one of his heroes, the reclusive Morrison, who died in 1971 after years of drug and alcohol abuse.

Now Cameron is 39 and works for Federal Express in Lafayette. He never fulfilled his ambition. But he got close to fame.

It was 1968 and Cameron's first Doors concert — at the Coliseum on Chicago's south side.

He remembers Morrison's blue shirt. The opening band. The playlist. Cameron rattles off the song titles — in order — as if he heard them only yesterday.

A collection of fuzzy, faded snapshots and a yellowed newspaper obituary of Morrison tumble from Cameron's leather folder as he talks.

The obsession with The Doors began in 1967 when Cameron was in summer school at Culver (Ind.) Military Academy. The Rockford, Ill., native was hanging out at a soda shop called the Shack listening to the juke box.

"I had never been grabbed by a song the way I was that day," he says. "It was 'Light My Fire.'"

Morrison's lush sound, Ray Manzarek's way with a keyboard and the lyrics by Robby Krieger were unlike anything Cameron had heard, he says. The next day

Jim Morrison
Died in 1971

he began buying Doors records. His approach to the piano, which he had played since childhood,

changed.

The Doors were his inspiration, the sound to copy.

The Chicago concert gave him a chance to get closer to his new heroes, the band that replaced the Beatles.

Cameron and a friend arrived at 1 p.m., about six hours before showtime. Finding an unlocked door, they walked in and immediately were recruited to help set up spotlights. Their pay: backstage passes and a chance to meet the band.

He forgot nothing about that day, nor his experience with The Doors. Every detail is vivid. He tells of the first meeting with Morrison as if he were writing the scene for a stage play.

"I walked down to the dressing room and Jim was with this fat guy in a black cape and four girls," he says. "I introduced myself and said something silly

See CAMERON, Page F2

Cameron

Continued from Page F1

like 'I really love your music.' And Jim said 'Thanks. I gotta get a beer.'"

Morrison's decline already had begun — he had gained weight, grown a thick beard, and his performances were sluggish under the influence of alcohol. But the music remained irresistible, Cameron says.

"The music was speaking to me," he says. "Talking about rebellion. Break on through and find out who you really are."

Cameron's $60-a-week job included unloading coffin-sized amplifiers from U-Haul trucks in Chicago, Minneapolis, San Francisco, Los Angeles and Mexico City.

It lasted three weeks.

By late July, Cameron had returned to Rockford. He missed his girlfriend, Kathy, and was ready to play his own music. He had learned enough about The Doors and his hero, Morrison.

Plans for a music career never blossomed, Cameron says. While living in Los Angeles, Memphis and Bloomington, Ind., he earned

minimal wages playing piano, but his Federal Express job paid most of the bills.

Cameron admits that he knew The Doors "only a little bit." But a little bit was enough. Cameron hesitated before seeing Oliver Stone's film biography, The Doors. "I have my memories," he says. "I didn't want them corrupted."

He went anyway.

After seeing the movie he concludes the director got most of the story right. What is missing, Cameron says, is the incredible conflict between Morrison the performer and Morrison the recluse.

He knows. He was there. He can't forget.

And he can't forget a night in Chicago when he stood next to Morrison backstage as a concert hall throbbed with calls for an encore — Doors! Doors! Doors!

"There are only brief moments in our lives when we're really, really happy," he says. "What I'm trying to get over is the idea that THAT was the greatest moment of my life, carrying amplifiers for The Doors as a snot-nosed 17-year-old."

The senior editor of Lafayette, Indiana's newspaper, The Journal & Courier, is Ms. Julie Doll, and I would like to thank her for giving me permission to use the "Roadie Can't Close The Doors" article. I appreciate your generosity very much. Thanks also to Judith Cebula, who wrote the article.

115

PART THREE

THE Q-95 CAMERON/
MANZAREK INTERVIEW

– 16 –

December 11, 1984

More than fifteen years after I had toured with the Doors, I arranged a two-way telephone interview with Ray Manzarek and myself, broadcast on Indianapolis rock station Q-95. The program aired on a Sunday evening, conducted by an affable enough deejay named Steve Church. My girlfriend Brier accompanied me.

CHURCH

So, now we're on with Doug Cameron. Doug was the first official assistant road manager of the Doors, in 1969. Welcome.

DOUG

Thank you, Steve. Nice to be here. Hello, Q-95, and hello, Indianapolis.

CHURCH

Doug has promised to give us some racy stories about life backstage with the Doors, but first, let's get right to our callers, who have been waiting. Okay, let's see…Q-95, hello.

CALLER

Hi, Steve. Hi, Doug.

DOUG

How ya doin'?

CALLER

Man, what was it like workin' with Jim Morrison?

DOUG

In a word, heavy.

CALLER

Morrison was really into drugs, wasn't he?

DOUG

I've read that earlier in the Doors' career—like '67, late '66—Jim was known to be a little high on hallucinogens before a concert, but when I worked with them, really, all they requested at the dressing room was just a lot of beer, and Jim just knocked down a lot of cans of beer. He really didn't smoke too much Mari hooch, as far as I know. I think it kind of put him on kinda a weird death trip. It made his body feel real weird, and I also think Jim was more enamored with alcohol because it was more of a social form of recreation or enlightenment, or whatever. He liked that you could go into the liquor store and throw down a five dollar bill and buy a bottle of something.

CALLER

Okay, but have you ever heard of him doing acid?

DOUG

Oh...

CALLER

With a hairy buffalo, though?

DOUG

I never really heard of the two together. I know that he did all sorts of different things in huge quantities, but as far as whether or not he ever attempted that particular combination, I really couldn't say.

CALLER

Okay, do you think, if he was still playing music today and he and the Doors were together, do you think they would be heavy metal, or what do you think they would play? Still the Doors' style?

DOUG

That's a tough question. I think that it would definitely come across as the Doors' style because I don't see how they could help but come across as the Doors. I think they probably would have done a couple of blues albums. I think they would have done a couple more poetry albums, and—who knows?—they might have even gotten into some jazz. Robby has been into some jazz in L.A., and so it's really the sky's the limit, but I'm sure it would have been good. Okay?

CALLER

Okay, thanks a lot.

CHURCH

I appreciate your call.

What about his relationship with his girlfriend, Pam? Now, he knew Pam before he became a "big star" and his relationship with her was kind of strange, wasn't it?

DOUG

Well, I think it was strange for Pam because Jim was, not incredibly, what is the proper word? He didn't really have a lot of faith in the word "fidelity" or whatever. I don't mean to be brash or anything, but Jim was involved with a lot of women, understandably, in his position, and I think it was difficult for him to just be with Pam exclusively, you know? Traveling as much as he did. But to my knowledge…

CHURCH

There are some stories, though, about him being very violent toward her.

DOUG

He, well, that's part of Jim. When he was drinking a lot, he was kinda violent, you know? Get the hell out of the dressing room, you know? Who needs you? Get your rear end outta here. I'm kinda cleaning that up a little bit, but then, when he was sober, he was the nicest guy in the world. I mean, terrific.

CHURCH

Any stories about his backstage exploits with women? Surely there must be some, especially from that period.

DOUG

Well, I know that on occasion—and I know this from what I heard, I was not there by any means—but apparently he was with some German film queen or film star, and they got a little gassed on something and got into cutting their veins and letting the blood run into cocktail glasses and drinking the blood.

CHURCH

Oh, boy!

DOUG

Yeah, it was out there. And Jim woke up in the morning and was all covered in dried blood, and he just kinda freaked out and went back home. He was into experiencing everything he could, probably short of a capital crime.

CHURCH

Huh!

Now, when you guys were out on the road, I assume, when the show was over, Jim just didn't go back to his hotel room and fall asleep.

DOUG

No.

CHURCH

What sort of things would go on after the shows?

DOUG

Well, it just depended. Jim might go to the airport and get on a jet for New Orleans. On one occasion it felt like he wasn't having enough fun. So he said, "Well, I have to go somewhere that I can have fun." So he went to New Orleans for a week after a show. When we played Chicago, he went to Hugh Hefner's place with the rest of the band and, you know. Of course, with any musician, you know it was Presley or a lot of people, you play until one in the morning. It's gonna take you until dawn to calm down and relax and get to sleep. That's intrinsic to all musicians, you know. That happened to me, too. It takes you all night to unwind, and when you've got twenty thousand people out there, and—of course, that never happened to me—but I can imagine, you know. I've played for a couple hundred people, and I mean it's an awful lot of energy you get charged up with.

CHURCH

What was it like with the fans backstage during that period? Well, you know, usually the concert promoters try to keep fans away from the backstage area, but it rarely happens that, and I'm sure… Well, what was the situation backstage?

DOUG

Well, with the Doors concerts, usually the security was very heavy because, of course, Jim was virtually a genius at crowd control. He kinda studied a little bit of that in school, and that kinda relates also to the one gentleman's question who called in a few minutes ago. Why are the Doors still in the public limelight, so to speak? I think one of the reasons was that Jim had such a charismatic control over people. And it's just kinda worn into the 1980s. I think in a way, Jim's still around. I think Jim haunts a lot of people. I don't know. It's kinda the way it is. Jim used to haunt me, but I think I'm getting over it.

CHURCH

Any other great stories from that period? Or odd stories? You mentioned that you had some stories that you weren't sure you could use on the air, but what the hell?

DOUG

Well, there are a couple that involve Ray, and I think Ray is gonna be on in a while. I probably shouldn't bring those up. I don't think Ray would be thrilled. But, well, just like one time we, well, that night at Sergio's De Club, Mexico City, we got a little gassed on what Jim called Morrison Specials. I think they're just rum and whiskey, or I mean Coke and rum. It's been so long ago, but we ended up going back to Parque de Los Principes, which was the villa we were staying at, and Jim and I endeavored to spend the rest of the evening till dawn practicing racing starts in the swimming pool there, after we found out we both swam the same events in high school. We were both on the high school swim teams, one hundred freestyle and two hundred yard or, no, excuse me fifty yard freestyle and one hundred yard freestyle. And we just talked about a lot of things. He was going to get a club together in L.A. called the Albatross, and, thinking back on that name, you know, "the Albatross"—I kinda feel like he said that because he had an albatross around his neck, just like the Ancient Mariner did. I don't know if you've read that poem, "The Rime of the Ancient Mariner" by Samuel Taylor Coleridge.

CHURCH

Certainly.

DOUG

I think Jim did have an albatross. John Densmore described it as like a hundred or two hundred pound medicine ball that Jim just carried around on his shoulders all the time. I mean, he was just so heavy, you know, and none of us really knew why.

CHURCH

Hmm. You keep mentioning that he was—you keep comparing him to Dionysus. Why? I mean, that implies that he was sort of an evil character.

DOUG

I think that ties in, yeah. I don't think that Jim was any saint. I don't think Dionysus was either. But, well, Jim was all things, except maybe chaste. And you can just paint him any color you want. I think he was good, I think he was evil. He endeavored to be everything he could be, and whatever he was was fine because he was doing it. It's just the name of the tune, I guess.

CHURCH

Okay, we'll play a song that probably should be our Sunday Night Live theme song, and we'll be back with a phone call to Ray Manzarek. Ray Manzarek is in Los Angeles. He was a keyboard player with the Doors, and he'll be on the air with us shortly.

* * *

CHURCH

This is Sunday Night Live, and you can ring us up using your very own telephone—239-1060—and telecommunicate with us here on Sunday Night Live. We're here till one thirty. Doug Cameron, here in the studio. He was assistant road manager with the Doors for some years ago, back in 1969 actually, when the band was at its peak. And on the line we have Ray Manzarek, who was then keyboard player with the Doors. Ray, welcome.

MANZAREK

Well, nice to be here.

CHURCH

First, the story about the new album, *Alive She Cried*. Is it true that somebody found these tapes, supposedly long lost tapes that nobody was aware of, in a vault somewhere, or on a shelf, and sold them for a thousand dollars?

MANZAREK

Yes, actually, Doug did that. Doug Cameron was the guy who found them, and he called me and said, "Ray, I've got these tapes." And I said, "Oh, that's great, Doug."
"There's just one problem, Ray. I want a thousand dollars for them."

CHURCH

Now, now—seriously, now…

MANZAREK

And, fortunately, I didn't have to pay him. It was a bad check. So, ha-ha, Doug. The joke's on you. But he was a lot of fun on the road. Doug was a laugh riot. *(Laughter in the background.)* Actually, we owe Doug a lot. He was a great guy.

CHURCH

No, seriously, about the tapes now…

MANZAREK

Seriously? Okay, seriously, he's not a great guy. *(Lots of laughter in the background.)*

CHURCH

Nobody ever said the job was going to be easy.

MANZAREK

It's not easy. No job is easy. *(Laughter)* Anyway, we hired this detective… Now, the tapes, the tapes were lost, yes. But, back to the tapes, the tapes were lost after we did the poetry album, Jim's poetry album *An American Prayer*. And we listened to a bunch of the tracks and took "Roadhouse Blues" for the *American Prayer* album from one of the concerts we did in Detroit. And then the tapes were put on a loading dock and were to be sent back to the storage facility. And somehow, when they went back to the storage facility, they got totally mislabeled and misplaced. And completely disappeared, and it was like *Raiders of the Lost Ark*. They were filed away with thousands and thousands of other boxes with the wrong label on them, and it took us ages to find the damn things. Finally, we weren't charged a thousand dollars. We offered to any of these storage facilities in L.A.—we weren't sure where the thing was—where all the tapes were. We said, "Look, the first person who locates these tapes, there is a thousand dollar reward." Well, two days later, boom, an enterprising young man had gone through all the tapes at one of the storage facilities and said, "Listen, I've got seventy tapes here that don't correspond to the label. I don't know what they are. Come on down and listen to them. They might be what you need. Take them back to the studio, check them out. If they're what you need, give me my money." And, sure enough, that's exactly what they were. Lo and behold, about a year ago, they finally turned up. So we went to work on them and put them into the studio and did a lot of EQing and a lot of ddl's and harmonizers. And everything was well recorded originally on eight track and sixteen track by Paul Rothchild and Bruce Botnick, so we had had some good stuff to work with, and just brought it up to state of the art fidelity.

CHURCH

Now, you re-recorded some of your keyboard parts. Is that not true?

MANZAREK

I had to fix a few things. I have to confess that I did make a few clams. You play live, and there are some things that you go, "holy bejesus, who the hell played that?" You know, it was probably Doug's fault. You know, I'm trying to play, and he's there alongside of me. "Hey, you want a beer? How about a beer, Ray?" *(Laughter)* "You want a cigarette? Something stronger to smoke, Ray?" Doug, leave me alone, will ya? Of course, you know, you hit a wrong note.

CHURCH

Of course, I suppose onstage you're probably, especially during that period when things were, I gather, a bit crazy, perhaps you weren't always thinking about the performance itself.

MANZAREK

Well, you weren't always thinking about the chord changes. Let me put it that way. There were other things like physical safety for your own physical wellbeing. If any of you get to see the video for "Gloria," there's a—we just finished a video and it's just premiered on MTV on Friday, and it's got some of the actual Doors riot footage at concerts going on. So you will get some idea if you watch the video of exactly what went on onstage. So, there were a few times when I didn't always hit the right note.

CHURCH

Why, you say riot footage, do you mean that literally? I mean, did people actually storm the stage and...

MANZAREK

People, yeah, you'll think it's kind of bizarro New Wave punk rock concert done, you know, somewhere in some crazy place in Los Angeles. But in actuality it's, you know, 1968/1969 footage. Some of it's from New York. Some of it's from Cleveland. Yeah, people would go crazy.

CHURCH

All right, now the big question all of us here are wondering about. Did Jim really unzip his pants in Miami?

MANZAREK

Is that what you're all worried about in Miami?

CHURCH

No, here, in Indianapolis, is where we are. And we are very concerned about it. Absolutely.

MANZAREK

Are there any women there, or is it all men?

DOUG

There's a female here, yeah.

MANZAREK

Are the girls worried about it, or just the men? *(Laughter)*

CHURCH

I think everybody in the city is concerned about this. I would say all mental activity, I'd say all mental activity here in the city has come to a standstill while we're pondering the question.

MANZAREK

They're waiting to know whether he did it or not?

CHURCH

Yes.

MANZAREK

You know, I can't really answer that question. I mean, I was there, but I don't know. I don't know. This is just like the stories of Jim in Paris. What happened? Well, I don't know. I mean, I don't know if anybody knows, you know? I think that's one of the wonderful things about Morrison. Nobody knows for sure.

CHURCH

Was Morrison…Would the band have been the band without Morrison? Could you guys have made it go? Or was he essential?

MANZAREK

No, he was essential. Of course, absolutely, absolutely essential. I mean, without Morrison, we're nothing. I mean, Doug didn't even buy *Carmina Burana*, for God's sake. *(Laughter.)* Or about what Ray Manzarek did as a solo artist, you know?

CHURCH

Well, now, you're doing all right as a solo artist. You've had some success.

MANZAREK

Hey, with all the—yeah—if anybody—thank God for Doug's sister. *(Laughter)*

CHURCH

We were talking earlier about the new album, and...

MANZAREK

I just made, I did *Carmina Burana* with Karl Orf and Phillip Glass. Karl Orf wrote it and Phillip Glass is the producer and Ray Manzarek is the artist. I know that doesn't mean much in terms of John Mellencamp Cougar. *(Laughter)* But sort of on an intellectual level, it's kind of important *(Laughter)* in the overall scheme of things.

CHURCH

Now, you'd better watch it. John listens to this show.

MANZAREK

Is he there? Give him my best, man. People have suggested that perhaps he could play Morrison in the movie. *(Laughter)*

CHURCH

Interesting thought.

MANZAREK

Yeah, it is—interesting thought.

CHURCH

Okay, back to Jim. I know you've been asked this question at least five thousand times, but...

MANZAREK

Well, maybe not.

CHURCH

I've got to ask the question. About Jim—what made him go? Why was he certainly one of the most enigmatic characters in rock and roll? Because we don't know enough about him, because he, you know, he either committed suicide or died, or whatever…

MANZAREK

Or disappeared.

CHURCH

Or disappeared?

MANZAREK

His own death.

CHURCH

Whatever.

MANZAREK

Did it in Miami, or didn't do it in Miami.

CHURCH

That's right. That, of course, is the most important question. But what made this guy go? Why is it, years from his death, we're still listening to his music, we're still curious about him?

MANZAREK

What is *is* about Morrison, you know?

CHURCH

Yeah, now let's…

MANZAREK

Not exactly a question a lot of people have asked, but it's like it's not a question, and I mean there is no real answer I can give to… He was a unique individual, strong, dynamic personality, driven. You know, he was totally possessed when he was onstage. He would go into what would amount to almost a hypnotic trance, you know? It's like a different person would emerge. Offstage he was quiet, withdrawn, kind of shy. And when he got onstage, he would just become Dionysus. He would become a…he would go into a shamanistic Dionysian frenzy, and he would become a different person—sort of a sensory enhanced, kind of into a—for want of a better word—a conniption fit, you know? An hour and a half conniption fit. This guy would be gone, but he would be gone in a kind of controlled manner so that he would lead the audience into this state of heightened awareness, and to this place where time would stop. Where the revolution of the planet would stop. The only thing that would be important would be the music that was going on, the fact that you were there in the audience. The Doors were making the music, and the audience was there, and that's all that mattered. And Morrison was the center, the focus of the whole thing. We made the music behind him. The audience was watching him from the front, and he just stood in that spotlight and commanded twenty thousand people to just pay attention to him. He had the power.

CHURCH

Now, is it true, or is it not true, that he sort of got into music by accident, sort of sideways? That he considered who read philosophy and such, and…

MANZAREK

Exactly, he was. He was the poet. That's exactly what he was. He was a poet, a filmmaker. He was an artist. He wasn't a musician, and that's where John and Robby and I came in. That was our function in the band. Jim was the word man. We were the bird men, we made the music. We made the sounds that surrounded and enveloped his words and his singing. And one Door without the other, you know, Morrison was, of course, the center of the focus of the whole thing. But without any one person, the Doors wouldn't have been the Doors.

CHURCH

Is it true that somebody had to force him on, almost force him onto the stage for the first time? *(Laughter)* No, I recall, I think it was in Sugerman's book that—and we had Jerry Hopkins on here a few weeks ago, and he was talking about this—that some other person, perhaps it was you, that had to…

MANZAREK

Yeah, he didn't want to go on the first time we played, the first gigs we played at the London Fog on the Sunset Strip in Los Angeles. Jim would turn his back on the audience. Fortunately, the London Fog was the kind of place that, if he *did* turn his back, it didn't matter because the audience usually consisted of the go-go girl on the opposite wall in her cage *(Laughter)*, a butler and a waitress and, you know, one drunk who was draped over the bar. Or two sailors who had come in looking for girls, and there wasn't a soul in sight. So it didn't really matter that Jim had turned his back on the audience and would just sing to the band. It took him a while to gain the confidence to turn around completely and face the audience. But, boy, once he did, he really got the hang of that very quickly—just completely took over.

CHURCH

Hmm. Now, Doug was telling me that there was a lot of, I guess you could say, racy backstage stories, but he was reluctant to tell them because some of them involved you, and he didn't want to say anything about you that...

MANZAREK

Well, that was decent of him.

CHURCH

And so I'll ask you directly to perhaps relate some of those backstage stories.

MANZAREK

You mean the stories between me and Doug? *(Laughter)* Are those the ones you're asking about? I'm not going to tell those stories. Are you kidding?

CHURCH

I think these related to...

MANZAREK

You promised you wouldn't tell! *(Laughter)* Listen, I'm not a kind of kiss and tell guy. Doug said he wasn't either, so forget it. We're not going to get into those.

CHURCH

We're not going to get any of that racy stuff out of ya, huh?

MANZAREK

I'm not going to tell any—it's Sunday. This is not blue Monday.

CHURCH

But this is an adult program. We have...

MANZAREK

This is a family show.

CHURCH

We have a bona fide X rating, and all the kids are in bed.

MANZAREK

What are they doing there? *(Laughter)* Well, listen, there are all kinds of stories. *(Laughter)* I mean, I'm sorry. I'm not going to go into some of the more scatological stories here, you know? It's the usual kind of thing, you know? Has to do with consumption of massive quantities of controlled substances, and, you know, the relationships between men and women, boys and girls. You know, things that people have been doing together, and touching various parts of their bodies—as my mother would call them—the dirty parts. You know, people would touch each other's dirty parts.

CHURCH

Well, that sounds like you guys had a lot of fun on the road.

MANAREK

It was a lot of fun. It was a lot of fun. I mean, Doug would keep you in stitches. *(Laughter and sigh)*

CHURCH

Okay, well, if that's all we're going to get. Hell, I was hoping to record all this stuff and sell it to *The Enquirer*, but…

MANZAREK

Uh, uh, uh. *(Laughter)*

CHURCH

No such luck, huh?

MANZAREK

I'm not telling those stories. You can't do that sort of thing. We're not the kiss and tell type.

CHURCH

Okay, Doug, do you want to…you've got the opportunity to be heard on big time radio. Do you want to ask Ray any questions yourself?

DOUG

Yeah. Can you hear me there, Ray?

MANZAREK

Yeah, I sure can, Doug.

DOUG

Hey, good. No, I was just curious as to whether or not, well, you know, just basically, how you feel about James Douglas after all these years. I mean, I know on occasion you're kinda reluctant to, you know, talk about those feelings, but…

MANZAREK

Yeah, well, yeah. Well, you and I have talked a lot about it and, I mean, actually what we should have done is taped our phone conversations.

DOUG

Yeah, I'm hep. We could have written a book.

MANZAREK

Doug and I have talked a lot about it over the years in long distance phone calls from Indiana to Los Angeles.

CHURCH

I suppose the thing that is most confusing to those of us who have not tasted, you know, that kind of huge success, is why a guy who had what you would think any guy could possibly want, you know, everything from financial success to obviously—he could have nearly anything he wanted with regard to almost anything that's available to human beings. Why would a guy who had adulation from people, who had everything anybody could want, why was he such a wreck, and ultimately, why did he—essentially, I guess—take his own life, whether or not it was suicide? He took it, perhaps, by over consumption and over-living, or whatever, you know? What would make a guy do that sort of thing?

MANZAREK

Well, let's think about terms of human existence. Maybe you're not supposed to have everything you want, you know? Maybe it's not in the cards that you have everything you want. Because, if you have everything you want, then what's left? What's the driving, motivating force then?

(GAP IN TAPE OF PROGRAM)

MANZAREK

Maybe I should stick around for a while then. Maybe *that's* what happened to Morrison.

CHURCH

Are you proposing *that* seriously? That perhaps he's...

MANZAREK

I'm proposing *that* as a key to every person's life. Of course I'm proposing that seriously. You're not intended to have everything you want. Because, what do you want anyway? You know, it's kind of a childish ego that wants, you know? Life is to immerse yourself into this planet. and to savor the very nature of the soul of this planet. Not to satisfy your childish wants. You know? Desire? That's not the key to existence, and if you do satisfy those childish wants, then you're like dust—blow it away, man, get outta here. Go someplace else.

DOUG

Well, you know, Ray, I feel like sometimes it was possible that Jim was kind of uncomfortable on this level of existence.

MANZAREK

That's very possible, man.

DOUG

You know...you know a lot about astral projection.

MANZAREK

Exactly. Very possible.

DOUG

But, I remember talking to Corky Courson one time about Pam and Jim, and I guess one time Pam just down with Jim and said, "Listen, why do you get so out of your mind all the time? Why do you drink so much?" I guess his initial response was, "Well, all of the classic poets did it, you know? I'm just staying in line with them." But, in the next breath, I think he said something like, "It's the only way I can stand myself." So, I don't know. I don't know if that's true or not.

MANZAREK

Yeah, I've heard a couple of other people offer that idea. I find that a little hard to believe. I mean, he was a terrific guy, you know? I mean, a guy looking that good. I mean, if you look at *The Illustrated History of the Doors*, the new picture book that's out, I mean, there are some photos of this guy and, my God, what a handsome devil.

CHURCH

Let me ask, you know, was that—I guess I have to direct this question to Ray—actually because you knew Jim before he was a big superstar. Why did that situation occur? I mean, was he like that before he was famous, or was it a result of his being so famous that people would react to him that way?

MANZAREK

Well, people always...It's fifty/fifty. He certainly had the power, you know, and he had that magnetism about him. He was a great guy, and was very good to look at, and he was a lot of fun to be around. But when you knew who he was, and a famous person walks into the room—Jagger. They project onto the person their own worship of that person. Holy cow, look—there's Jesus Christ! Oh, my goodness gracious, what a terrific guy he is. So it's fifty/fifty. You project onto another person. But, in the end, you know, everyone is a human being. We're all human beings, and all human beings have the power to attain cosmic consciousness. I mean, that's the whole point of it. It's to find out that everybody on the planet is one. If anybody out there in Indianapolis is listening, Ray Manzarek is offering oneness. Anybody into oneness there? And if there are any Atonists, please write.

CHURCH

Optimists? Did you say optimists?

MANZAREK

No, I didn't. *(Laughter)* No, I said Atonists.

CHURCH

Atonists?

MANZAREK

I think Atonists will know who they are. If there are any, look at the sun, Aton.

CHURCH

Can you…is this a secret thing that you can tell us about, or…

MANZAREK

No, hardly. No, it's a very public thing. Unfortunately, it ceased to exist about 3,500 years ago, so…

DOUG

Sun Ra.

MANZAREK

There aren't a lot of Atonists around. The golden scarab. Doug, you've got the golden scarab.

CHURCH

Well, you've got me…

DOUG

Yeah.

CHURCH

You've got me curious. What the hell is all this about?

MANZAREK

Well, it's probably one of the new…it would be one of the new religions. One of the coming religions of the new millennium. After we finish up this millennium and get onto the next millennium, we'll probably be getting into Atonism and various other forms of sun worship.

DOUG

Right.

MANZAREK

The solar god, the deity of the sun.

CHURCH

Ra power.

MANZAREK

Ra power, yeah. *(Laughter)* Iggy pops up from ra power. *(Laughter)* I like that. Ra power. That's good, man. That's what it is. That's going to be the salvation of the planet, and the key to the energy, and harnessing the solar power.

DOUG

The golden people, right?

MANZAREK

So as soon as we do that, it will clean everything up. We stop with the atomic and the oil and all that business.

DOUG

And I'll tell you, Ray, I promise I'll pick up a copy of Carmina Burana and everything will be fine. *(Laughter)*

MANZAREK

Hey, I just want you to listen to it, man. You can listen to your sister's copy. You don't have to go out and get one.

CHURCH

Okay, we've got "Riders On the Storm" coming up. Now, that is a song that Jim wrote, correct?

MANZAREK

Yes, that's right. Well, Jim wrote most of the songs and, you know, certainly most of the lyrics.

CHURCH

Right, any…

MANZAREK

Although Robby did get a lot of songs started. "Light My Fire" was brought in basically by Robby Krieger, and the Doors' communal mind went to work on it. And, you know, most of the songs developed that way. It almost didn't matter who really wrote the song. It's what the song became after the song was brought in and everybody put his two cents into it. Of course, Jim was the main lyricist.

CHURCH

Did you…were you guys reading books during that period?

MANZAREK

Oh, yes, yes, yes, yes. Also for the audience, I would like to offer another suggestion. Read books. *(Laughter)*

CHURCH

Well, now, from a rock and roll performer, that's a rather strange statement. Because I don't imagine many read books, actually.

MANZAREK

Well, I think that's one of the problems. *(Laughter)* For God's sake, read books!

CHURCH

What sort of books?

MANZAREK

Kids still read books, don't they?

CHURCH

What sort of books were you reading at the time?

MANZAREK

Oh, boy oh boy. It's hard to say.

CHURCH

Nietzsche?

MANZAREK

It doesn't really matter. Whatever appeals, you know? Just reading absolutely anything at all is worthwhile reading.

DOUG

Right.

MANZAREK

Any reading is better than no reading. The philosophical, cosmic consciousness stuff, you know? It's overly intellectual. Hard to get people really interested in those kind of things, you know?

CHURCH

Any insight into the lyrics of "Riders On the Storm"? Now, I suppose at one level, it's just a piece of pop fluff. Is that all it is?

MANZAREK

Well, it's...there's a killer on the road. *(Laughter)* Hardly pop fluff. *(Laughter)* You guys must be pretty heavy there in Indiana.

CHURCH

No, no, we play lots of pop fluff, and I plead guilty to that. I didn't mean that in a derogatory fashion.

MANZAREK

No, no, no. I understand that. Of "riders on the storm" and "into this house we're born." "Like a dog without a bone, an actor out on loan." It's kind of a song of desperation. It's a song saying there's nothing, there's nothing but death awaiting you on the highway, you know, this highway of life. What's out there? What's out at the end of life? It's death. It's a killer on the road. It's the reaper, man. The reaper is out there waiting for you at any moment. But the only salvation you have is, "girl you gotta love that man. Love him while you can." And that's...love is the only thing that will keep the reaper, keep the darkness, keep the light in our lives. Keep the darkness out. It's the light. It's a love song. But it's a dark, gloomy song. And, interestingly, it's the last song he ever recorded. The last song he found on the album. I think it was the last time he was in the recording studio, and is truly the last song. It's the last song the Doors put down, the last one on the album, the last song Jim sang. And if you listen very closely at the end of the song, you can hear the whisper voice. Jim overdubbed his own...he overdubbed himself whispering the lyrics to the song. And you'll hear him in there. It's sort of a ghostly kind of voice. It's almost a premonition of Jim's death.

CHURCH

It was indeed prophetic and, Ray, thank you for joining us in the proceedings here.

MANZAREK

My pleasure, man. My pleasure.

CHURCH

Goodnight.

MANZAREK

All right. See you later, Doug. Take care, buddy.

DOUG

Thanks, Ray. Bye-bye.

(MUSIC: "Riders On the Storm")

CHURCH

We'll be back with a little more from Doug Cameron with regard to the Doors and some of your calls on that subject. And then we move on to a free-for-all phonegoria. First, here's some Doors from the new one, *Alive She Cried*. This is a remake of the old rock and roll song "Gloria." Q95.

(MUSIC: "Gloria")

CHURCH

And we're back telecommunicating 239-1060. We'll be spending another fifteen minutes here with Doug Cameron, who was assistant road manager with the Doors, back in their peak in 1969, knew Jim Morrison and Ray Manzarek. We just concluded a conversation with Ray, who was keyboard player with the band and was the, I guess you could say, straight head that kept everything together when Jim would rather have it falling apart, I suppose.

DOUG

Yeah, Ray was always the one that appeared to be like a college professor, possibly of theology or some type of metaphysical endeavor. But, basically, you're right, and more specifically, musically you are right. Because Ray played the key bass, of course, and was basically responsible—oh, no pun intended—for the delivery of the music. And Robby and John basically keyed off of what

Ray was doing. So, in a way, it was a little bit similar to the way the Stones go about music. Which is, they basically just follow along with Keith Richards and, of course, Keith plays a heavy rhythm guitar. And that's why the Stones have such a nice guitar sound. Because they work at getting two guitars playing the same chords and links, and they get that "righteous" guitar sound.

CHURCH

Hmm. Okay, now, are you gonna leave this Atonist business…did I pronounce that correctly?

DOUG

That was correct—Atonists.

CHURCH

Are you going to leave this a big mystery, or are you going to try to explain it a little bit?

DOUG

Actually, Steve, I think it would probably be better to just leave it in the mysterious category. To tell you the truth, I can only refer to the actual meaning of the word. But I think it's important to leave it unanswered because I think that very few people in their lives are ever really asked a real question. I know I've only been asked one or two in my entire life, and I think that maybe some people out there need to be challenged and have to deal with the real question.

CHURCH

Okay. Anything you say. *(Laughter)* We've got a few phone calls here, so let's move into them now. Hello—you're on the air.

CALLER #1

I'm a musician calling Doug. What do you think about modern music today flashing back, using poetry mixing…well, I'm not into any kind of New Wave. I've been having these flashes of thoughts. I've been writing them down and I want to know what you think.

DOUG

Well, you've really asked two questions. To answer the first one, as far as what I think of today's music—and I'm thinking as a musician to you, musician to musician—a lot of it kind of bores me, really. If I was going to go back into music, I think I would try to keep it as simple as possible, with as few effects as possible, because I want what I do to be a true representation of my creative self. As far as your other question on your getting flashes of creative poetry, I think the best thing you can do is make sure you keep a pen and paper with you, and when you get a flash, get it written down. Start writing. Write down your flashes. Write down your ideas. Write down a lot of things because it helps. It's like therapy. It makes you feel better, and it gives you another perspective on yourself. And, when you have enough things written down, maybe you'll have a story or a poem, and then you can find some good musicians that care about art, and maybe you can get something done.

CHURCH

I wish you the best. Q95, hello.

CALLER #2

All right. Now, first up, I want to ask two questions, okay? First up, are you going to be playing the Inn tonight? Some of the Inn?

CHURCH

I wasn't planning it, no.

CALLER #2

Okay. Then, my second question is, in part of the song he says, "Father…" He says, "Yes, son…" "I want to kill you." Kind of a poetry song also. But, and then he says, "Mother…"

CHURCH

I hope you're not going to say what I think you're going to say.

CALLER #2

Yeah, I know. But that's what I want to know. What does he say, or can you say that?

CHURCH

Well, it's quite obscene, so actually we probably shouldn't repeat it. I think it's clear what he…I think most people know what he says, and he does say it.

CALLER #2

Okay. But I just want to make sure what he said.

DOUG

Yeah. It was a four-letter expletive…

CALLER #2

Oh. Okay.

DOUG

...that he used rather frequently in concerts. But it's not...it was taken out of some of the albums.

CALLER #3

Am I correct that that was the theme song to *Apocalypse Now*?

DOUG

Yeah, they used that for *Apocalypse Now*, and there is a little story behind that. I'd heard the tune, you know, a number of times, and then when I saw the movie I thought that they'd used a different version because I heard some vocals over the TV set that I'd never heard before. And what they did was...it's the same song as on the first album, but they re-EQ'd it in the studio, they remixed it. So they brought out more vocals.

CHURCH

Good night. One final question for Doug, and then we'll do a free-for-all phonegoria, which means you can call us up and bend our ear on any subject. Hi...

CALLER #3

I've been a Doors fan for about five years now and, you know, after reading the book and listening to his music, he kinda scares me. And I wondered, back when the Doors were a group, if any of the members, or Doug himself, was scared of Jim Morrison.

DOUG

That's a very good question, and I'm glad that someone asked about it. I think the band was afraid of what he was doing to himself. And I think you have to treat Jim Morrison with a lot of care when you are listening to his music and trying to learn about him, or listening to his message, because I do think, as I've said before, he was all things. He was sometimes good, he was sometimes evil.

* * *

ALMOST FAMOUS:
THE DOUG CAMERON BANDS

This is a chronology of every band I either formed or performed with in my futile quest to become a rock 'n' roll star. I did, however, have a lot of fun.

1. The Drew Dobson Band (Culver Military Academy—Summer 1968)
   (Drew Dobson was the son of General Dobson, the Superintendent of Culver. We played "Light My Fire" among other rock and R&B tunes. I played a rock organ. It was my first gig ever. I got paid $15. Man, did *that* feel good. After his father's death in 1997, Drew spun out and developed a career in Alabama as "The Gentleman Bandit." God bless you, Drew.)

2. Itchy Brother (Weissmansdorf, Germany—Spring/Summer 1971)
   (My first band. We never played anywhere, but we drove the Germans nuts with our loud practicing. Paybacks are a bitch!)
   Drums: Mike "Dough Boy" Kauffman
   Guitar: Don Impink
   Bass Guitar: Neal Butler
   Piano/Vocals: Doug Cameron

3. Terra Firma (Bitburg, Germany—Fall 1971—Spring 1972)
   (A G.I. band, and a damn good one. We played gigs at ancient little clubs in the Eifel Mountains, and once in Holland. Many stories…not enough time.)
   Vocals: Paul Black
   Bass: Phil Davis
   Drums: Bruce Lohman
   Guitar: Leo Jones
   Guitar: William Todd
   Keyboards/Vocals: Doug Cameron

4. Sneed Hern (Kokomo, Indiana—Summer/Fall 1972)
   (The first real band I created. We played a number of gigs around Kokomo and also performed on the David Letterman "Clover Power" show in Indianapolis. We actually wrote and performed one or two interesting originals among some Steely Dan, Doors and R&B.)
   Rhythm Guitar: Denny Miller
   Guitar: Doug Schultz
   Drums: Danny Crude
   Piano/Organ: Dan Leap
   Bass: Bruce Oberdorf
   Various Keyboards/Vocals: Doug Cameron
   Fuzz Bass: Larry Smith

5. Fin (Jacksonville, Florida—Spring/Summer 1973)

(We practiced for hours and hours every day in this little dump of a house on the edge of a swamp. There were growling animals inside the walls of the practice room. We played twice in a nightclub down on Jax Beach and made peanuts. I split in the middle of August to go to school at Indiana University in Bloomington, Indiana. I don't think I was ever so relieved to leave a place. Ah, college. What a concept!)

Guitar: Leo Jones

Drums: Will Carasquillo

Bass: Al ?

Farfisa piano/Hammond organ/Vocals: Doug Cameron

6. Scratch (Bloomington, Indiana—Spring/Summer 1975)

(We played the Bluebird nightclub in Bloomington, usually making $180 per night. We made many dollars for the owners, but couldn't even pay our own bar tab. We were pure cannon fodder.)

Trumpet/Flugelhorn: Dave Miller

Alto Sax/Flute: Rich Oppenheim

Drums: Bob Austin

Guitar: Jeff Boyd

Bass: Dennis Neal

Vocals: Janice Russell

Keyboards/Vocals: Doug Cameron

7. "The Mickey Bands"

(Named for Mickey Mouse. In New York, musicians would call these gigs "club dates." One such gig was the Westbury Underground, where I played piano for the lunch crowd. The place was usually totally empty. Fellow "mickey" musicians included Don Long, Don Bemis, Don Peipher, Gene Benjamin, Tug Beale, "Dave Joe" Barrett, Steve Johnson, Dave and Rhonda Welch, Dave Grissom, Sandy Williams, Don Campbell, Brian Kearney and Russell Flynn.)

8. Innersound (Kokomo, Indiana—Summer/Fall 1976)

(We played Chick Corea-type music, but only performed a few times. The hottest band I ever worked with.)

Guitar: Dwight Sills

Bass: Thomas Glenn

Drums: Vernon Marshburn III

Electric Piano/Synthesizer: Doug Cameron

9. Renee Miles & Doug Cameron (Indiana University—Spring 1977)

Renee is a jazz singer with an incredible range. We performed as a duo in a coffee house/lounge lizard format in many venues on campus. We did a lot of ballads. I miss working with her.

10. David & the Rockabilly Rollers (Los Angeles—Fall 1978-Spring 1979)

    (This band tried to capitalize on the rockabilly resurgence that was happening in L.A. and other places in the late Seventies. I don't know WHAT THE HELL I was thinking, but the other guys in the band were pleasant enough, and I was somehow convinced that this was the right path to take. It wasn't. The upside of being in the band was that I realized I was a damn good entertainer. Also, we did have opportunities to play some famous clubs in L.A., such as the Troubadour, and up in the Valley (San Fernando), we played a gig at the Palomino Club. We met Waylon Jennings that night. Another night, I met Charlie Hodge. Man, that cat Charlie Hodge looked LONELY. Elvis had been dead about two years at that time. I left this band and took my new wife, Barbara, back to Indiana with me. Our daughter, Leslie Tennille Holzer, was born January 3, 1980. The Captain was not around.)

    Vocals: David Wallin

    Drums: Steve Kopperman

    Guitar: Kent Alexander

    Bass: Gary "Smugheimer"

    Piano/Vocals: Doug Cameron

11. Roadhouse (Bloomington, Indiana—Fall 1979-Spring 1981)

    Trumpet/Vocals/Various Percussion/Jim Beam: Jim Kirkman

    Drums: Greg Vance (variously)

    Drums: Kevin Newcomb (variously)

    Drums: Candy Pinkston (variously)

    Various Keyboards: Doug Cameron

12. Doug Cameron at Eddington's Barbeque Pit, a piano bar in Bloomington, Indiana. (Fall 1987-Summer 1988)

    Played 10-20 gigs, maybe more. Some very good times.

13. Sharon & the Bikemen (Bloomington, Indiana—Fall 1988—Spring 1989)

    (A band that played a few club dates around town. We had fun and made, again, the usual pittance. At the end of one gig, Tom Moeller told me, "Man, you are the biggest ham I've ever worked with." I took that as a compliment.)

    Bass: Steve Johnson

    Guitar/Sax: Tom Moeller

    Guitar: Dave Baas

    Drums: Robby Helms

    Vocals/Screams: Sharon Beikman

    Piano/Vocals: Doug Cameron

14.Almost Famous (Rockford, Illinois—2008—Present)
(Currently working on occasion. Greg is the author of *13 Days of Terror: Held Hostage by al Qaeda Linked Extremists—A True Story*. His story aired on the National Geographic Channel's "Locked Up Abroad," April 15, 2009.
Drums: Greg Williams
Keyboards/Vocals: Doug Cameron

* * *

EPILOGUE

This whole book is an epilogue. I was one of the kids who got to go with the Pied Piper of Hamelin. I was not the pudgy kid who was left behind when the mountain entrance closed.

There has been a profusion of books about the Doors. Unless Robby Krieger decides to write his memoirs, the only other book on the horizon would be Vince Treanor's. As of now, that project "is still in dry dock," as he has alluded to me. If it is ever published, it may well be the last gasp by anyone who was actually on the road and in the studio with the Doors. Until then, is my account the last word? Could be. But I doubt it.

When I was last in Los Angeles—July 2008—I was really hit by the massive change in the social vibes of the city. The spirit of '69 had disappeared into the ether, taking the young man that I was then with it…a loss that was so hard to bear. The Doors are gone. Jim is gone. Having the Doors as an existing, functioning band was like having the opportunity to climb Mount Olympus and hurl thunderbolts with Zeus. It was like crossing over into another realm of consciousness. But Ray—you didn't need acid to take the trip. The Doors were one of the smartest bands ever. I saw evidence of this time and time again. There were hundreds of bands in Los Angeles in the late Sixties, but only one rose to the top: The Doors. They eventually "slipped the surly bonds of Earth." And they are timeless. The music and the lyrics speak for themselves. The Doors will live on, the same as James Dean and Marilyn Monroe.

But rock and roll today? There's no comparison between 1969 and 2009. Forty years ago, rock music *meant* something, *said* something. So what if so many of its icons—Jim Morrison, Janis Joplin, Jimi Hendrix—had their flaws? They were thinking, feeling human beings, and they made the audience think and feel. Today it's all about technology, and the "heroes" are the iPod and the Blackberry. The technocrats have taken over. *1984* has finally arrived—about twenty years late, but it is now here. *1984* IS HERE! Computers have taken the aspect of human caring and responsibility out of the equation. Now, if something goes wrong in your life, BLAME THE COMPUTER. *It's not my fault!* Oops! We just dropped a nuke on Moscow. BLAME THE COMPUTER!

In the final days of the Doors' existence, Jim sounded so unhappy, so tired. He really was trapped by his own words. He also crossed the line from which most never come back. "Once you cross over me," the line says, "you truly will believe in your own fame, your own greatness, and your imagined immortality."

Jim Morrison. What can I say? I loved the *image* of Jim Morrison. He was one of the few original thinkers I have ever met. He lived his beliefs. For me, hanging around with Jim was like hanging around with Dionysus, or even Jesus. The cat seemed spectacular at the time. Did I love Jim Morrison, the man? How could I? I barely knew him, but I like to think we were friends. Forty years later, I feel sorry for him. Yes, he's famous now, but was the cost worth it?

You decide. I was one of the moths drawn to the flame of the Doors, and now I can finally put the experience into proper perspective, let the fire die.

I wonder if anyone truly knew Jim Morrison, a man who spent many a night curled in a fetal position, having just puked his guts out on the floor of the West Hollywood workshop. Still can't get that rug—and its "polka dot" pattern of stains—out of my head. How much unhappiness drove him?

When Jim died, I think his family was crushed. He could not say "no" to anyone except his loved ones. His mother called him all the time. She even called when we were having a huge, extravagant poolside breakfast in Mexico City. Evidently she had that number because Jim wanted her to have it. I don't believe he ever saw his father after 1965. I think this is sad, but it is clear to me that the late Admiral Morrison really pissed Jim off. Jim returned the favor on March 1, 1969, at the Dinner Key Auditorium in Miami. Thanks to Jim's alleged "lewd and lascivious" performance, the senior Morrison lost his chance to become the youngest Fleet Admiral in the history of the U.S. Navy. The schism between Jim and his father was the cutting edge of the Generation Gap. Jim once bought an expensive set of golf clubs for his attorney, Max Fink, with a card that read: "For the only father I've ever known."

Every few years, I have what I call "a Jim Morrison dream." In each of these, I'm hanging around somewhere, and Jim shows up. Or I'm at a concert, with good seats, and the Doors are playing. One time, he and I were sitting at a bar. I looked over at him and saw him wearing a leisure suit! I couldn't believe it, and the vision actually woke me up.

Once, I even had a new Doors tune come into my head, and it wasn't bad. Of course, when I woke up, it vanished back into the cosmos. The most recent of these dreams was possibly the most telling of all. The actual dream was non-specific, and I never saw Jim. In it, I was talking to someone from California who lived near Santa Monica. I asked this person about Jim and was told that he was getting by, not performing any more. But people had seen him. When I woke up, I cogitated about the dream for a moment, and as I became fully alert I realized...but Jim is dead. I wish somehow, some way, someone could have set the "freedom man" free so he could have lived longer. I miss him.

A former acquaintance of mine in Rockford, Illinois, once remarked, "Doug, you know, you never got over the Doors." And he was right. I never want to. Did I *love* the Doors? Damn straight.

Okay—everyone who loves the Doors, take a deep breath and exhale slowly:

This is The End.

Untitled #2

The man who sings the blues
Is singing from his heart.

He sits at his piano,
Late at night,

And cries his tunes
To the moonlight.

He's lost lovers,
And he's lost heroes.

He's laughed till he's cried
Over memories only he knows.

Brier Frasier

POSTSCRIPT

THE SEARCH FOR MY ORIGINS

The big mystery of where Doug Cameron came from existed, for me, for approximately twenty-nine years. Fortunately, it did not take that long to track down my biological mother. All the detective work took about six months.

The record of my adoption was in the Howard County courthouse in Kokomo, Indiana, and I knew that thanks to the efforts of my sister, Mardi. However, she could not have access to the files. What to do...what to do?

Dan, an old family friend, was an attorney in Kokomo. I called him and explained the situation. Dan said he would look into it and get back to me. His return call came one week later. After he made me promise to never reveal his name (I promised), he gave me the vital information—birth mother: Margie Allison.

All right...now how do I find a trail that has been cold for twenty-nine years? The first step was the Kokomo High School library. There I found two pictures of Margie Allison. Now, how do I find her? A sudden flash of inspiration shot through my brain—check the 1951 Kokomo phone book. All old directories are on file in public libraries. I cross checked the ancient Kokomo listings with the latest ones and---BINGO! One name came up in both: a guy named Allison. I called him and said, "Listen, I'm an old friend of Margie Allison. I haven't seen her since high school, and I'm in town for only a brief time..."

"Oh," he said, "you mean Margie Dosier." He told me she worked at one of the local hospitals.
"Man, that's great! Thank you so much for your help!"
"You bet. So long."
Cowabunga! I said to myself. *My, oh, my..."*

I called the hospital's insurance office and said I wanted to speak with Margie Dosier.

"Well," said a woman who was not Margie Dosier, "what is your last name?"

I realized immediately that she thought I was calling about an insurance claim and wanted to plug me into the appropriate clerk. Not wanting to reveal my true identity, I said, "Johnson," completely unaware at this time that Johnson was my biological father's surname. Talk about a coincidence—I could just as easily have said Smith or Jones. I was put through to a second woman, also not Margie. I told her I would call back later.

The following day I decided to eliminate all of the middle women. I drove out to the hospital, found a pay phone inside and called the insurance office. I asked to speak with Margie.

"Margie Dosier?" the woman at the other end asked.

"Yes." A few seconds passed, each feeling like a year.

"Hello," said the somewhat earthy, curious voice. "This is Margie."

"Yes," I said. "Hi, Margie. This is Doug Cameron. How are you?"

"I'm fine," she said, no doubt wondering why I was waltzing around the issue. "Who is this?"

"Um, well, it's kind of hard to explain."

"Oh?"

"We spent some time together, many years ago."

"Well, when was this?"

"It was in Terre Haute. This is your son."

There was a pause at the other end, followed by a big sigh. Then Margie said, "I'm so glad you called."

"Me, too, " I said, choking up.

"Where are you?"

"I'm right here."

"Where?"

"At the hospital. By the east door."

"I'll be right there."

I'll always remember that it was a sunny morning. I looked down the hallway to a pair of glass doors. The doors parted, and a woman with a glowing smile walked toward me, her arms outstretched. She was as tall as me, and had some meat on her bones. Talk about a bear hug… We couldn't avoid crying. It was one of the most important moments in my life. Now the mystery was going to be solved.

Margie is not my mom. I've never called her mom. I call her Margie. My mom is Barbara Cameron Edwards and I love her more than every star in the universe. But I am damn thankful for Margie Allison Dosier. The woman has grit, and she's got a heart of gold. Margie did what she thought was best at the time, as is the case with almost every human being when faced with a very difficult decision.

When I think of Jim Morrison I'm still amazed that he detached himself from his family. He did what he thought was best at the time. He got the fame. I still have my family, and my life. Honestly, I don't give a damn about fame anymore.

* * *